No Shoes Allowed

—Delightful tales in a dream world setting. This book will make even the most serious landlubber want to chuck it all and head for the tropics—
Dockside Express

—A wry and engaging glimpse inside the luxury charter yacht trade in the Caribbean. In its pages, you can feel the sun shining and those steady winds blowing, hear the lilt of Caribbean English, and slip into island time—
Pacific Yachting Magazine

—Carries you back to the freewheeling pioneer days of the Caribbean yacht charter industry—
The Caribbean Compass

—Entertaining and enjoyable reading about a relaxed lifestyle—
Latitudes and Attitudes Magazine

—Fascinating, humorous and different. A welcome and uplifting breeze of fresh air. Leaves the reader longing for more—
Mirrors

No Shoes Allowed

by
Jan J. de Groot

EMERALD POINT PUBLICATIONS
21909 - 3rd Avenue, Langley, BC
V2Z 1R8 Canada
Phone (604) 533-7185   Fax (604) 533-7194

NO SHOES ALLOWED

This 3rd edition published 1999
by Emerald Point Publications

ISBN: 0-9683547-0-X

Printed in Canada

*"One ship drives east and another drives west
with the self-same winds that blow,
'Tis the set of the sails and not the gales
which tell us the way to go."*

Ella Wheeler Wilcox

This book is dedicated to the Yachties, those brave men and women who fearlessly traded their secure life in the establishment for the 'hardships' of labour on pleasure yachts plying the tropical waters of the Caribbean Sea.

All stories told in this narrative are true. In some cases the names of certain individuals have been changed to protect the innocent. In other instances, names were changed to protect the guilty. Wherever possible, permission has been obtained from guilty parties to put their part in these stories in print. To those I have not been able to reach, I can only say, "Tough luck! But, I love you all, wherever you are! Fare well and God bless!"

This book is about the sea, about the Caribbean Islands, about the charter trade, about boats and about people, mainly about people. It begins like this....

Prologue

It is customary to take one's shoes off when boarding a yacht. The reason is obvious, shoes track dirt onboard which will be ground and scratched into the varnished or scrubbed teak-wood components by the bearers of the footwear. In bygone days, sailors would spend endless hours polishing teak decks with holystone. Nowadays, modern recipes for concoctions such as Teak Bright allow the sailor to remain in the upright position rather than having to go down on his hands and knees while tending to this labourious task. Nevertheless, on a well kept yacht, still, a lot of time is devoted to keeping the decks in spotless condition.

For the skipper of a luxury charter yacht there is another, hidden advantage: the charter clientele often consists of government dignitaries or politicians in high positions, executives in charge of large corporations, millionaires, heirs of large fortunes, and movie stars, some of which have very big egos. Sometimes these individuals are under the impression that the charter contract gives them ownership of the yacht and crew. It is important to establish a line of command the very instant these power houses step on board. After all, there can be only one captain in charge.

Nothing demolishes a big ego more than the insistence that the newly arrived party remove their shoes when boarding. This is done in a courteous manner of course.

"Welcome on board, did you have a pleasant flight? The crew will take care of your luggage," and then, firmly, "Would you please take your shoes off before boarding?"

This is received with an instant downcast of their eyes towards their feet.. The self importance draining downwards simultaneously. Sometimes a puzzled look towards the captain and a hesitant, "Really?"

"Yes, no shoes allowed, you are in barefoot country now. Might as well let it all hang out, set the poor suckers free."

Soon, hesitantly, the shoe removal begins, releasing their feet and now cheerfully discovering that indeed, they have arrived in the land of fun and sun, the harnesses undone. Soon they stand there, smiling, fully-dressed in tailor-made gear, but with shoes in hand, toes wriggling, twisting and feeling a bit awkward. Carefully they climb on board, subdued but happy and acknowledging the captain's authority.

Believe me, it works every time.

From the Merchant Fleet to the Charter Scene

We were in the Atlantic on a southerly heading, destination Pernambuco, also called Recife, on the coast of Brazil. After that, we would be calling in at various ports along the east coast of South America, discharging and taking on new cargo. The ocean had calmed down considerably. The ship's bow rose and fell easily in the long swells left by the gale we had encountered the previous day and well into the night.

She was a handsome ship, rated at about twelve thousand tons and measuring some five hundred feet in length. We carried general cargo and up to twelve passengers. I was proud to serve on her. I felt particularly good this very minute since it was the first time that I was in command. The fact that my command was only for the duration of this watch did not matter. As far as I was concerned, right now, I was the Captain. The Captain, the real Captain that is, had been on the bridge most of the previous day and night during the gale.

As a junior officer I was delegated to stand watch with the Captain. The other junior being supervised by the chief mate. When I came on watch this morning, ten minutes before 0800, the Captain was already there, waiting for me. As I entered the bridge, the Captain was standing near the telegraph on the opposite, starboard forward corner of the bridge. His eyes trained on the horizon ahead of us. His back turned to me. Arms relaxed behind him, the right index finger hooked through his left thumb. He turned as he heard me enter. He looked tired, the strain of his long presence at the command post showing.

"Ah, there you are!"

"Good morning, Captain," I replied and looked around for the Chief Officer who was to be spelled of his watch.

"I sent him to his bunk," the Captain said, interpreting the puzzled expression on my face. "And," he continued, "I'll be following shortly. So, you'll be on your own. You think you can handle that?"

Wide-eyed I looked at him, absorbing the full extent of his implied order. He trusted me with the responsibility of the running of the ship! My imagination raced. I saw myself like Hornblower pacing the deck, anticipating the next move of the enemy, bringing the guns to bear, making ready for a broad side for the final coup de grace. The Captain's voice brought me back to reality.

"Well, did you hear what I said?"

"Yes, sir, of course sir," I blurted out, and hastily added, "I can handle it, sir."

"Right then, if anything out of the ordinary

happens, you call me immediately, understood?"

This time I replied with an immediate; "Yes, sir!"

For a brief moment the Captain gave me a pensive look, then he walked towards the door and as he stepped through said, "Eriksen is in the chart room. He'll brief you on our status before he signs off."

As the door fell closed behind him, two seamen arrived via one of the bridge wings. They were the relief for the rest of the watch complement. During the night watches, the watch included three seamen: one on steering duty, one as lookout, and one as standby. Every hour they rotated. During the day, the look out was not required except, during poor visibility such as fog or while navigating in close quarters. During daylight hours, the third man worked his watch time on deck, participating in the daily routine of maintenance, doing whatever needed doing under direction of the Boatswain.

I conferred with Eriksen, the other junior, who brought me up to date on our present position, course and other traffic. There were no other ships reported in our vicinity. I signed my name in the log and Eriksen departed. Then I went to the steering station, verified the course indicated on the slate, actually a box with interchangeable numbers painted on pieces of plywood, and looked on as the new helmsman took over from his predecessor. I heard him repeat the course as he took the wheel and trained his eyes on the compass.

The ship was equipped with an auto pilot, but we rarely used it. The captain felt a crew was more alert without artificial aids. He did not trust the radar either. This was the time before electronic gadgets. Our radar was one of the first to be installed in a commercial vessel. Nowadays it would be classed as an antique. The contraption had been fitted just before our departure. It was being regarded as a mystical object from another planet, capable of sinking the ship if the wrong button was pushed. A whole cabin below the midships was occupied with the secret parts of the thing, tubes, dials, wires, knobs, transformers and other incomprehensible items. Only Sparks, our radio operator, seemed to have some sympathy for the machine. When we had entered the Elbe on our way to Hamburg a few months ago, the ship was slowly crawling ahead while enveloped in thick fog. Both the captain and the chief officer took turns looking at the radar screen and then stepping outside on the bridge wings, trying to see through the fog and listening for fog horns from other ships. Eventually, the captain took one more look at the radar screen and then said, while walking over to the telegraph and ringing the engine room for a dead stop, "We'll stay right here until the fog has lifted." So much for our radar! The instrument had been avoided like the plague ever since.

I stood on the port wing of the bridge scanning the fast expanse of ocean around me. "Nothing out of the ordinary," I mumbled, "just water, no traffic." A movement aft, on the poopdeck some 200 feet away, caught my attention. With mild curiosity I turned my glasses to the activity. Someone was throwing objects over the side. I adjusted the binoculars to get a better look, and to my amazement saw a man throwing several loafs of bread into the water. This was followed by a whole Edam cheese and four packages of butter. I shouted to him. The man looked up and I waved him to come to the bridge. I waited for him at the top of the outside stairs leading to the outside wing of the bridge. The man climbing the stairs was the deck boy whose duty, amongst other things, was to serve the meals, wash the dishes and clean the mess room of the seamen, who were accommodated near the stern of the ship.

"What the hell were you doing?" I said, agitated, "Throwing good food away?"

The boy nervously shuffled his feet and then said, "Uh, uh, the Boats told me to, Sir"

"The boatswain told you to throw whole loaves of bread, cheese and butter over the side?"

"Uh—Yes Sir," he stammered.

"For God's sake, why? Has it gone bad?"

"No Sir, something to do with the Union, Sir," he answered nervously.

"The Union?" I exclaimed, "What has the Union got to do with it?"

"Don't rightly know, Sir," he answered, hopping from one foot to another.

Realizing this was getting me nowhere, I said, "Alright, find the boatswain and ask him to come to the bridge," and then, realizing I had not been made Captain yet, I continued, "No, forget it, I'll find him myself, you go back to your work."

With this, the fellow rapidly disappeared down the stairs. I looked at my watch and noticed the time. Eleven hundred, six bells, one hour until the end of my watch. I turned and stepped from the wing through the door into the inside workings of the Bridge compartment. I told the seaman on duty at the helm to keep a good look out and left in search for the boatswain. As I exited the midships onto the main deck, I spotted a seaman busy with a paintbrush. "Where is Bakker?," I asked. "He's in hold number three, shoring up some of the cars that shifted during the gale." "Thanks," I said, remembering the Chief Officer's comments to the Captain when relieving him from the previous watch. Something about checking on the cargo of automobiles, bound for Buenos Aires, at first light. "Right on," I thought, "He was right, they did shift."

The ship had five holds, two aft and three forward. Number three was located right under and forward of the bridge which was four levels up. I proceeded to the hold and noticed some of the wedges had been taken out and a corner section of the tarpaulin and the covering boards had been removed. I peered down the hole and saw men working in the cavity. I stepped over the hatch coaming and descended down the iron rungs leading to the various levels of cargo space. Soon, I came upon a group of men who, under the scrutiny of Boatswain Bakker, were busy working with cables and come-alongs.

"That ought to do it," Bakker said to the men and then to me, as he noticed my approach, "Some of them shifted a bit, but even a typhoon won't budge them now."

"Good," I answered him, watching the seamen gather their tools and climbing out of the hold. "Tell me," I said when the last man disappeared,

"What's this about you telling the deck boy to throw bread, cheese and butter over the side?"

Bakker looked at me with surprise. "How do you know about that?" And after a moment's pause answered his own question, "The rat fink," referring to the deck boy.

"I saw him do it," I said, "Did he lie?"

"No he didn't. I told him to."

"To throw away good food? Why?"

At first I thought he was going to tell me to mind my own business, but instead, obviously embarrassed, he shrugged his shoulders and replied, "For years we've been fighting with the ship owners for our rights; working conditions, accommodation, wages, and so forth, including good grub. The union demands from the owners that certain quantities of food supplies are made available to the crew. That amounts to a certain amount for each crew member. You know what I mean— so many pounds of butter, so much cheese and so forth." He watched me with speculation.

"Y-e-s," I said slowly, "So what?"

"Well, you see, we're actually getting more than we need."

"So?"

"Well, uh," and then he blurted it out, "If we return it, the owners would shorten our rations, which is something the Union wouldn't like, would they?"

Disgust made me hesitate for an immediate response. The Boatswain was several years my senior in age. The second world war was still fresh on our minds. Anyone who had lived in occupied territory during the war years would remember the suffering and eventual death of many caused by hunger. If I remembered, certainly the Boatswain would remember. I had been a teenager during those years. He was married with children and would have had to provide for them.

After I had gathered my thoughts, I said, "Boatswain, what you just told me is appalling. You remember the war, don't you? Didn't your wife ever have to tell you there was nothing in the house to prepare a meal with, that the last slice of bread had been eaten several days ago? That there would be no ration tickets until next week, or the week after that? You remember that, don't you? And now, now you're throwing food, good food, over board because this is what the Union wants?"

Embarrassed, he looked away, his face flushed.

"No more food over the side, OK? If the Captain finds out he'll have a fit. Either let the men eat until they burst or have it taken back to the stores!" Having said that, I turned around, climbed out of the hold and went back to the bridge to finish my watch.

During another voyage we were held up in Buenos Aires for three whole months because of a strike of the dock workers. We were to take on grain which, with the modern machinery available, could have been loaded in a few days. The dock workers only showed up on Sundays because then they received double pay, or when it rained, when they did not have to work at all, but still were paid for their presence. In contrast, later, when we discharged this same cargo in Madras in India, the ship was emptied in four days. The dock workers there did this without the fancy equipment which was available in Buenos Aires: two men holding up a burlap bag, a third scooping in the grain with a shovel and the fourth carrying the full bag on his shoulders while climbing out of the hold via the iron rungs.

A subsequent voyage held us for three weeks, due to litigation and Union negotiations resulting in fines, because the third mate removed a forklift truck, for which the driver could not be found, from the area where we had to deposit cargo.

These incidents, combined with a dock strike caused by our complaint to the local Police of some other Port, about a trio of longshoremen who were caught opening crates and making off with the contents, lead me to re-think the future of the Merchant Marine, and in particular my future in it. I could not see how shipping companies could continue to operate under these conditions. Now looking back, I think my thoughts had merit. The large merchant fleets of countries such as England, Holland and the United States have virtually disappeared. Those ships, or what is left of them, are now flying Monrovian, Panamanian and other flags of convenience. What happened to the seamen who were employed on these ships?

Regardless of the Union incidents which flared up every now and then, I stayed with the merchant marine for some time. Promotion came fast those early years after the war. Shortage of personnel in expanding fleets, high demand for the shipping of cargo encouraged by a flourishing economy, allowed an eager young man to gather his stripes quickly. I was no longer a Junior when

I was on a ship berthed alongside the wharf in Santos.

The wharf at Santos was different from most in that the entire structure was built of timbers laid on wooden pilings. It stretched for a couple of miles along the waterfront and about three hundred feet inwards, towards the land. On this vast expanse of platform, large hangars and sheds were erected which contained precious cargo, offices, equipment, etc. Also placed on the platform were numerous, great mounds of bananas awaiting shipment to other ports. In amongst this, workers, trucks and other equipment were busying about.

Our ship was tied to the wharf in the usual manner. Two breast lines, two stern lines, one spring line running from the stern to the dock forward and one spring from the bow to the dock, running aft. In addition, a few lines were secured at about midships. Our spring lines were of a type called, 'Hercules', comprised of a combination of steel cable and manilla rope. They were heavy and immensely strong, as the name suggests. Due to a shortage of cleats mounted on the wharf, our springs were tied to the pilings, the pilings providing a very secure object to tie to, since they in turn were fastened to and part of, the entire wharf and loading platform.

We had completed our business in Santos. The hatches were battened down and the ship was ready for sea. All mooring lines except one breast line, one stern line and the springs had been removed and stowed on board. The third officer was in charge of the lines on the fore deck, the fourth mate was at his station on the aft deck, and the Captain and chief officer were on the bridge. Since my watch as second officer was about to begin, I was present on the bridge also, to relieve the chief officer as soon as the ship was free and off the dock. The chief officer took the intercom and said, "Foredeck, let go all lines. Aft deck, let go all lines except the spring." This was soon followed by replies heard via the speaker. "Foredeck, all lines on board" and, "Aft, all lines on board, spring still on dock." The chief, standing by the telegraph signalled the engine room for a short burst astern. Soon the vibration created by the huge propeller could be felt. Then it stopped and the ship slowly went astern until the spring checked its way, upon which the bow slowly started to swing away from the dock. "Rudder midships," the chief said to the helmsman simultaneously ringing the telegraph for ahead slow. He nodded to me upon which I took the microphone off the intercom. I waited until I could feel the vibration of the propeller and said, pressing the button of the mike, "Let go aft spring." "Aye, aye," came the reply. A few moments went by, then some shouts could be heard, interrupted by the voice of the mate, shouting into the intercom, "She is stuck, we can't get her loose!," indicating that the linesmen on shore had been unable to slip the spring's loop off the piling. In the mean time, the ship had started to make way, ahead.

I must now take a moment to impress upon the reader the enormous forces at work when dealing with the sometimes cumbersome mass and weight of ships. Even a smallish boat, once underway, is not that easily stopped. The bigger and heavier the ship, the longer it takes to bring its movement in check.

"What the hell!," exclaimed the chief officer while ringing for dead stop and then astern on the telegraph. "Too late!" I heard the Captain say who was standing in the back ground behind us. An agonizing crunch could be heard when the Hercules spring pulled the piling away from the dock. The ship was still moving ahead slowly. All of us now had our eyes fixed on the spectacle that unfolded on the loading platform behind us. Like dominoes in a slow motion replay, we saw the next piling go down, than the next and the next and so on, pulling with them the wooden timbers which formed the base for the dock. This was followed by a huge pile of stacked bananas which slowly submerged into the dark depths under the docking platform. Then a forklift truck and then a shed containing an office together with desk and clerk slid down with the crumbling timbers. People shouting, running for safety, not knowing which way to turn. Suddenly the whole of the platform shuddered as if shaken by a giant monster lurking underneath. A ripple soon to develop into what seemed like a wave, travelled the entire extent of the wharf, buildings collapsing, trucks being swallowed into the murky waters under the wharf. Chaos, as far as the eye could see!

In the mean time, the ship had finally lost her way and had come to a full stop. The chief officer rang the engine room to stop engines. Soon the vibration created by the reversing propellers, ceased. Dead silence on the bridge! Only the shouting, yelling and crashing coming from the shore could be heard. The Captain stood there quietly surveying the scene. He then took the mike of the intercom out of my hands and said to the mate on the aft deck, "Mister, is that spring on board yet?" The speaker crackled, followed by a hesitant, "Yes Sir, she's free and on board." "Good," said the Captain, and directing his order towards the chief officer, he continued, "Get us out of here as fast as you can, we'll let the agent deal with this mess." He was referring to the Company's shipping agent on shore. We were soon out of the harbour, headed for the open Ocean. Following subsequent discussions in the mess room, the consensus was unanimous about one thing: had we not left while we still could, we would have been held up in Santos for weeks, maybe months.

Well before the fleets had vanished, I resigned from the Merchant Marine, emigrated to Canada and had a go at being a land lubber. I entered the business world. I did alright in it, in the business world that is, but after my initial enthusiasm, my heart was in it no longer. I yearned for the sea.

One day I had to make a trip to our branch office in Vancouver. As soon as I had some spare time, I trotted off to one of the many marinas to have a look at the boats. Soon I found myself standing in my tailored suit and important looking briefcase on the dock of a marina near Stanley Park. I was studying a sailboat which displayed a "For Sale" sign. The boat was a ketch, a double ender with salty appearance, about 36 feet long. Two sturdy masts, bow sprit, baggy wrinkles, lazy jacks, good solid lines, sturdy rigging. The hatch opened and a head popped up, out of the small trunk cabin. A man squinted his eyes in the sunlight. His wrinkled face looked as salty as his boat. He peered at me and suddenly said;

"I used to wear a suit like that."

"Is that right?" I replied.

"Yeah," he continued, "I also used to carry a fancy briefcase, something like yours. I had a big house, two cars, refrigerator, TVs and the whole nine yards."

"What's the refrigerator got to do with it?"

"It's got to be bigger and fancier than the neighbour's, keeping up with the Jones', you know."

"Oh , I see," I said agreeably, "So, what happened?"

"Packed it all up, couldn't stand all the baloney."

"I know what you mean," I agreed. "I'm beginning to feel the same way."

"Ah," he exclaimed, slapping his hand on the cabin top, "You're coming to your senses. You wanna buy my boat?"

"Maybe, but what are you going to do if you sell her?"

"Fix up another one."

"I see," I said. "How much are you asking?"

"Twelve thousand."

"Hm, twelve thousand, sounds reasonable. I'll think about it."

"Sure," he said, "you do that." Having said that, he disappeared below and slid the hatch closed.

I walked along the dock a bit further, looked

at some more boats and then returned to the branch office of the company I worked for.

Several months later, business brought me back to Vancouver. After a good lunch in a waterfront restaurant, I found myself near the marina where my encounter with the old sea dog had taken place. I decided to take a look and see if I could strike up another conversation. The boat was still there, as was the "For Sale" sign, but the old codger did not appear to be on board. Adjacent to the boat was another sailboat on which a young couple were busy varnishing the capping rail.

"Hello," I said. "Do you know where your neighbour is?"

"No," the lady replied. "He left early this morning; we haven't seen him since." Looking at her companion, she added, "Have you John?"

"No," he agreed, "I don't know where he is, he should be back today though, cause when he goes away overnight, he usually tells us, so that we can keep an eye on his boat. Are you thinking of buying her?"

"No, not really," I said, "although twelve-thousand seems quite reasonable. He should have no trouble selling her for that price, don't you think?"

"Twelve thousand?" He scratched his head, "You must be mistaken, he is asking fourteen thousand."

"Really? I could have sworn he said twelve, not fourteen."

After chatting a while longer, we said goodbye and I returned to the office.

Several months later, business brought me back to the branch office. On the second day I made my now familiar stroll to the marina. The man was sitting cross legged on the foredeck, busy putting an eye splice in a length of line. He looked up from his work when I stopped by his vessel.

"Ah, it's you again. How goes the rat race?"

"Not bad, how are things with you?"

Shrugging off my question, he replied, looking at me pensively, "Yeah, well, you won't last much longer."

"What do you mean?" I said, laughingly, "Are my days numbered? Are you a fortune teller?"

He shook his head and laid down his tools. He shifted his position, and resting his elbows on his knees he looked me over. Then he said, "No, it isn't that. I can tell— those clothes, that briefcase, your heart isn't in it. When you stare at my boat, you have that look in your eye."

"Is that so?" I mused and changing the subject I asked, "How much were you asking for your boat again?"

"Fifteen thousand," he said, without blinking an eye.

"Fifteen?" But last time you told me it was twelve thousand."

"That's right," he said without hesitation, "and than I increased it to fourteen, and a few weeks ago I raised it to fifteen thousand!"

Making sure I had heard him right, I repeated, "First it was twelve, than fourteen and now fifteen thousand, but that way the boat will never sell?!"

"Of course, she will sell, I just haven't found the right price yet." And then he explained his novel sales technique.

"You see, it works like this, when the price

was twelve thousand, no one bought it because the price was too low. People figure that if the price is too low, the boat is no good. So, I raise the price. Eventually we get to a price where the buyer thinks he is getting something really special. Why do you think people pay more for expensive brands of merchandise?" Answering his own question he continued, "Because it sounds good and it allows them to show off to their peers. If it's expensive, it must be good!" He was silent for a minute, allowing me to contemplate his philosophy. "You should know what I am talking about, you got conned into that same rat race," he added, "just look at yourself!"

For several days the man's words rattled through my brain. I think I sort of agreed with him. In a way, he had put into words some of the doubts I had been carrying in my subconscious for some time. I could hardly wait until my next trip to the branch office.

About four months later I was down at the marina again. This time the boat had disappeared, but I observed the young couple, again busy, sprucing up their boat.

"Hi," I said, approaching them, "Remember me?"

"Oh, sure," came the reply, "How are you?"

After we had exchanged pleasantries I asked what had become of the old man and his boat.

"Well, you know, that's an interesting story. Do you remember that you said that the man had told you that he wanted twelve thousand and he had told us fourteen?"

"Yes," I said impatiently.

"Well, she is gone, the boat is sold and guess what, he raised the price again."

"Yes, I know, " I said, "he raised it to fifteen thousand."

"No, no, no, they hurried, the boat sold for SIXTEEN thousand dollars!"

A few years later I had bitten the bullet. No more suits and ties, no executive clubs, no hassle. I had bought a nice 55 ft. Yawl, which provided good live aboard accommodation and was able to take us cruising. How exactly I was going to accomplish all this I had not figured out yet, because I was now married and the proud father of two beautiful little girls.

We had all moved on board and were temporarily tied up at a dock in a downtown fisherman's wharf. I kept busy sorting out some of the gear which we inherited with the purchase of the boat. One cumbersome item was a wooden whisker pole that was meant to be used for the balloon jib. Nowadays these sails are called cruising spinnakers or genakers and who knows what else. The pole was heavy and about 35 feet-long, made of spruce and brightly varnished. It was a good looking thing, but it was also a pain in the neck, or feet, rather, since one constantly stumbled over it, no matter where on deck it was stored. I decided that it was more of a nuisance than it was worth and had temporarily put it on the dock alongside the boat. Eventually, I would figure out what to do with it.

One nice afternoon I decided to go for a stroll along the docks to look at some of the other craft that were located in the vicinity. Most boats were fishing vessels but here and there some pleasure craft were tied up as well.

On dock D, I noticed an interesting, small sail boat which had no rigging on it. The state of the vessel indicated that she was being re-fitted. I walked over for a closer look, when I noticed a man crouched down in the cockpit at work with a paint scraper.

"Hello," I said, "Nice boat you got there!"

The man looked up from his work and said, "When she's all fixed up, she'll be for sale. You wanna buy her?"

The man looked very familiar to me. I replied, "No, I already have a boat."

"Oh, which one?"

I thought I saw a flicker of recognition. "The one over there, " I pointed, "the yawl on C dock."

"Ah," he said, "What you gonna to do with that spar that's lying on the dock by your boat? I could use it, make it into a bow sprit."

"I don't know yet, I'll probably not be using it."

"You might as well sell it then."

"I guess so."

"How much?"

I thought for a minute. "Fifty bucks."

"Hm, eh— I'll think about it."

"OK," I said and continued my stroll along the docks.

A few days later, I was busy on deck when I saw the man coming up the wharf towards us. He stopped at the boat and looked at the pole which was still lying on the dock. I studied him from the corner of my eye, pretending I had not noticed him. I saw his gaze moving from the pole towards me. He scraped his throat to catch my attention and spoke up. "How much did you want for that spar?"

Without batting an eyelid I replied, "Eighty dollars."

"What?" he cried out, "The other day you said fifty."

"That's right," I said, "But nobody bought it, so I guess it was too cheap!"

"Damn!, he exclaimed, "I thought you looked familiar— teaching me some of my own lessons, hey?"

"Yeah," I agreed, "I am a fast learner."

"I'll say you are." He fumbled in his pocket and counted out 80 dollars. While doing so, he mumbled, "I better take it now before you increase the price again."

With this, he cracked a smile, handed over the money, picked up his spar and walked off.

That was my first encounter with one of the many colourful characters I was to meet in the pleasure boat industry. The Yachties, consisting of skippers and crew and the Dock Rats, who are in other ways scraping a living off the operation of pleasure boats. Later, this was particularly evident in the charter game in the Caribbean. There, Yachties with backgrounds from all walks of life and rebelling the regulations and pressures of the civilized world have created a lifestyle of individuality, away from the big cities and formalities dictated by society. In other words, they left the rat race and traded it for a life of adventure, open skies, clean oceans and warm winds. Some of them are doctors, advertising executives or owners of prosperous businesses. Others are blue-collar workers. All of them share the common bond of operating and maintaining their vessels in the best way possible. Some brought their own yachts, others are employed on yachts owned by people who have neither the time, the know how nor the inclination to run the vessel themselves. The yachts owned by absent owners are usually engaged in the charter business to offset some of the expenses, or for tax reasons.

Arthur Holgate, whose background I don't know, was one of those men. He built his own beautiful, steel schooner. The boat, called *Antares*, was, or is, some 90-feet long with a raking sheer and gaff rigged. Not the easiest type and size to handle with a small crew. However, Arthur, who was a very private man, decided that regardless of the benefits of having some capable hands on board, they also were a hindrance to the extent that they upset the meticulous manner in which he kept his vessel. If crew were kept on the vessel, they occupied cabins and brought gear on board, all of which required straightening out during and after a long voyage. Arthur decided he did not want to put up with this. He cleaned the boat thoroughly, put all the cabins in order with the bunks made, than sealed all the doors with tape to prevent dust from entering and proceeded to sail his large craft from South Africa to the Caribbean single-handed! He completed the voyage without fuss and when he arrived at the charter boat show in Antigua, after removal of the tape, his yacht was ready to be shown off to the charter agents for examination. Only while on charter,

Arthur would hire crew to cater to the needs of his passengers.

Cariad is a sailing yacht of around 100 feet in length. The vessel was built in the late 1800s and originally owned by Lord Dunraven. She actually was a J boat built for long distance racing. The yacht was in neglected condition when purchased by a South African industrialist who wanted to take a sabbatical from his business. The yacht was brought to Durban where the new owner started to rebuild her. At some stage during the restoration, the man's business started to develop some problems, forcing him to abandon his newly found project. He sold the boat to some of the hands who had been helping him with the restoration project. The helpers formed a partnership of four and resolved to finish the rebuilding and then take the yacht to the Caribbean to enter the charter trade. There was only one problem, none of them had any sailing experience, nor did they know how to navigate. But, this obstacle did not stand in their way. When the ship was ready to go, they entered the Cape Town to Rio de Janeiro race. The theory being, that this way they would be in the company of other boats and most of all, by just following the fleet, it would get them across the ocean and into the right direction. Once they were in Rio, all they had to do was head north along the East Coast of the South American continent. What they had not bargained on was the fact that when they arrived at the starting line, it was blowing a hooley. Forty knots plus! Not having any experience they

Cariad **charges across the starting line.**

did not realize that under those conditions one shortens sail by putting in reefs and not raising certain sails that might be carried away by the force of the wind.

Their enormous, gaff-rigged ketch arrived at the starting line with all sails set! Across the starting line they went, with all sails flying they were soon out of sight, many miles ahead of the racing fleet. It is a miracle that the whole kit and caboodle, sails, rigging and masts, were not ripped out of the hull. Fortunately, the next day, the winds abated to a light, gentle breeze which allowed the racing fleet to catch up and show them the way to Rio de Janeiro. By the time they arrived in the Caribbean, the entire crew were seasoned sailors and continued to successfully ply the charter routes with many a happy charter guest on board.

As time progressed, the original group of owners went through some changes and during the latter part of her charter career the yacht was run by a South African couple, Nick and Pat, who in 1983 took the yacht to Cowes Week. While the yacht was anchored off the yacht club, Pat was having a drink at the bar with some of the yacht's crew. Attractive, Pat soon became the attention of a dark-haired stranger who stood sipping his drink a short distance away from her. After some time had gone by, the man gradually edged his way over next to where Pat was seated. He casually started a conversation.

"Hello, are you here on a yacht?"

Pat turned to the stranger and answered, "Yes"

and then turned her attention back to her companions.

The stranger tried again, " Which one?"

"Which one what?" Pat asked, slightly irritated by the interruption.

Pat was unaware that her friends tried to discreetly attract her attention.

"Which yacht are you on?" He repeated.

"Oh, yes of course," replied Pat, now remembering the original question. She pointed towards the anchorage, "That one over there, the *Cariad*!"

"Ah, *Cariad*, yes, very nice yacht," came his response.

Pat agreed. "Yes, she is a lovely yacht. Are you on a yacht too?" Pat asked politely but really not all that interested.

Again one of her friends nudged her, a few giggles could be heard, but Pat paid no attention.

"Yes."

"Which one?"

"That one over there, the dark blue one, her name is *Britannia*."

Having said this, Prince Charles pulled his bar stool a little closer to Pat's.

In the early seventies I joined the ranks of the Caribbean charter operators through the purchase of a beautiful yacht called *Ring Andersen*.

The yacht *Ring Andersen* anchored at English Harbour, Antigua

Ring Andersen

Below decks

On deck

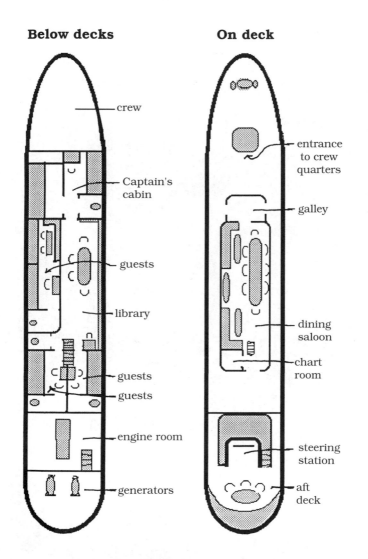

crew

Captain's cabin

guests

library

guests

guests

engine room

generators

entrance to crew quarters

galley

dining saloon

chart room

steering station

aft deck

The Islands

First Time Out

On Thursday, at three o'clock in the afternoon, I arrived in Grenada. The *Ring Andersen* was alongside the dock at Grenada Yacht Services. Except for one sea trial with her previous captain, some six months ago, I had not been to sea in her. I had received the telephone call a few days ago in Vancouver. David Collyer, the yacht's purser, rang from Grenada. The conversation went something like this;

"Jan, we've been offered a charter in Tobago, shall I take it?"

"What are the dates?"

"It's for ten days starting next Saturday."

"Next Saturday? This coming Saturday?"

"Yes."

"Is the boat ready?"

"Yes."

"Alright, take it then, I'll be down as soon as I can."

Dave rang on Tuesday. On Wednesday evening I boarded the Air Canada flight to Miami. From there with Eastern to Barbados and then LIAT to Grenada. It had been a tiring flight with long waits for connections, but here I was, on board the *Ring*.

David Collyer welcomed me on board and helped take my luggage below.

David had been in Grenada for several months, getting the boat ready for the new charter season. The *Ring Andersen* had recently acquired new owners (yours truly and a partner), and some changes were to be made to her interior. David was sent down to supervise the work and take care of the yacht's administration. I had known him for some time and as far as I was concerned a better person for the job could not be found. Besides being very capable and reliable, David was also one hell of a nice guy to have around. He was in his late twenties and his good looks and pleasant manner made him popular with the charter guests, especially the ladies.

Dave and I took a seat on the aft deck under the awning and he filled me in on the work that had been done and what preparations had been made for the forthcoming charter. As I expected, David had taken care of everything in his usual efficient manner. He then showed me the charter contract. The charter was a bit unusual in that the yacht was contracted to a large insurance company which was holding a convention in Tobago. The insurance company had booked the entire Mount Irvine Bay resort in Tobago for its staff, which consisted of several hundred employees. We were to take groups of 30 to 40 persons each day for a cruise along the Tobago coast. The contract read that the passengers would not be sleeping on board, we were to supply lunch at $3.50 per head and drinks at $1.00 each. The cost of lunches and drinks was over and above the basic charter fee. We were to bill the company separately for these extra expenses at the end of the charter.

"Well," I said to David, "that looks fine to me."

"That's what I thought," he replied. "This was arranged by Adrian Volney, the local charter agent here at Grenada Yacht Services."

"Hmm, looks like a good job, nothing is left out. How is the crew?"

"Fine, Jan, they're a nice bunch of guys and have all been on the boat for several years."

"Good, there have been no changes then."

I had met the crew once before, during the sea trials. They were all native Grenadians. Twin, the chef, had been working on the boat for some ten years. His culinary skills were known throughout the Caribbean. In addition, he was a good seaman and could pitch in when an extra hand was needed on deck. The locals have an uncanny flair for inventing nicknames. Practically everyone has one, which sometimes creates difficulties. Nicknames are so commonly used that a person's real name draws a complete blank. Ask for Jim or John and all you get is a vacant stare.

Twin was our chef's nickname, his real handle being Lauchland. One can see why his nickname is preferred. He is called Twin, of course, because he is one. Other members of our crew were Goblet, for Aubrey (our pigeon-chested steward),Cane Juice, for Raphael (Raphael was our bosun who once was caught on the prowl in a rum factory where he got thoroughly juiced), Mankind, for Rudolph (our forever friendly deckhand), Steambox, for Thomas who doubled as deckhand and did some engineering, (he started our air-start engine which sounded something like kshsh-voom, followed by, shekapooha, shekapooha, shekapooha.), J.P, for Vibert (our other deckhand, later our bosun, when Raphael left. He apparently had a Justice of the Peace for a grandfather).

Other nicknames of characters around the dockyard were Ants and Metric, two little guys, sometimes employed on the *Ring* as extra hands, and Hungry, a fellow who had incredibly large jutting teeth and thick lips. Another chap was called Ugly and believe it or not, there was a man named Double Ugly! Much later, I was to find out that I had been given a nickname too. At first I was referred to as Copperhead, later this was changed to Smoothies, (this, presumably, as a result of my disappearing hairline).

In the ensuing years I learned to really appreciate my crew. They were a terrific bunch of guys and most of them stayed with me for the next 10 years. They became family and their families became part of *Ring.* When Aubrey received a job offer from one of our charter guests, he left for the US and was replaced by his brother Dunbar. When Vibert had to retire as a result of a nasty accident with his motor cycle, his brother Rock, (Rochelle) took his place. Later, when *Ring* was sold and I left the boat, they all quit. With great difficulty I persuaded them to continue with the new skipper. Reluctantly they stayed, but only for a short period of time. This is West Indian loyalty for you!

Dave and I took a walk around the boat. I

talked with the crew and inspected some of the gear. Everything looked in order and ship-shape. It was about 5:00 pm and soon it would be dark. The sun sets early in the tropics and I wanted to leave that evening so that we could be in Tobago the following morning. I took a look at the charts and discovered that the chart of Tobago was hopelessly outdated. It had been printed in the previous century and lacked a considerable amount of detail. I imagined that things had changed in the last 100 years or so. The added difficulty was that Tobago lay out of the usual charter circuit. Upon questioning some of the local charter skippers, I could find none that had been there or had any up to date information. It was therefore imperative that we made a landfall in the daylight. Also, it would give me sometime to explore the area before we started taking the insurance people on board.

At 7:30 pm, *Ring's* engine was fired up and the mooring lines were cast off. Manoeuvring *Ring* is rather like acting as a tram driver. The ship has a variable pitch propeller. To change the pitch, one has to turn a large bronze wheel. A small bronze wheel operates the throttle. In addition to that, there is the vessel's steering wheel plus a large bronze lever which engages and disengages the clutch. A turn to starboard in close quarters is negotiated somewhat as follows:

Turn the steering wheel to starboard, crank the propeller pitch to forward, push the lever down to engage the clutch and then give her a quick burst of power by rapidly turning the throttle to open. Then, rapidly unwind the throttle, disengage the clutch, unwind the propeller wheel to full reverse, engage the clutch again, wind up the throttle and turn the steering wheel to port as she gains way astern. Then repeat again and again.

With all the yachties on shore sceptically watching the antics of the new skipper, secretly hoping that he would provide them with cocktail hour entertainment, we backed out of the slip, then turned in very tight quarters and motored out of the harbour, leaving the spectators behind deprived of their Happy Hour's gossip. *Ring's* engine went Sheka-pooh-a, Sheka-pooh-a, with the accent on the she. At 150 revolutions the engine pushed *Ring Andersen's* 220 tonnes at 9 knots. Out we went through the narrow channel entrance of the lagoon, then through the main harbour, out past Fort George and then out to the open sea.

I brought the ship around to the course I had drawn on the chart to clear the southern tip of the island. It was dark now, but Grenada's coastline could be clearly distinguished under the starlit sky. The angle we were steering in relationship to the coast did not look right to me. I glanced at the compass and then at the course I had written on the slate. The numbers corresponded. I rechecked the course line drawn on the chart against the printed compass rose. No, I had made no mistake. Again, I looked at the coast and compared it to the direction we were heading.

There's something wrong here! Must be the compass, I thought. I had seen another compass in the chartroom, one of those contained in a wooden box and portable. I pulled it out and took some bearings. Yep, the main compass was way out. I calculated the difference and adjusted the helm to the proper course.

Later, I was to find out that the ambitious crew, in order to varnish the binnacle casing, had removed the magnets which were screwed down to compensate for compass errors. When they re-installed them, they had not put them back in the right sequence. During the entire trip, we had to double check each course change with the chartroom compass.

When we passed Point Saline Lighthouse at the southern tip of the island, we altered course and headed for Tobago some 100 miles away in an easterly direction. We had a favourable wind so the sails went up and the engine was stopped.

Under the starlit tropical sky, I cast my eyes over *Ring's* decks. A steady breeze of 20 knots pressed her to a comfortable angle on a port tack. Her bow rose and dipped in slow motion to the Caribbean swell. She was clocking off a steady 10 to 12 knots, seemingly without effort. I could hear Twin busy in the galley. The occasional sound of laughter came from the foredeck where the crew were playing cards. With each whoosh of broken wave passing by, I could see the phosphorescent lights, created by millions of microscopic creatures, shoot through the ocean depths like a flash of lighting. An intense feeling of peace and well being overcame me. This was right, this is the way it is supposed to be. I patted the coaming of the steering station and mumbled, "We're going to be together for a long time old girl." As if to answer, *Ring* increased her heel slightly as the added pressure of a momentary increase in wind was caught in her sails. The yacht's movement was majestic.

The *Ring Andersen*, fondly called *Ring*, was 98 feet long on deck, including the bowsprit she measured just short of 120 feet. Her beam was 21 feet 6 inches. She was built of 4 inch oak and beech planking on 6 inch by 8 inch oak frames; she was massive and displaced 220 tons. Ketch rigged, the main mast towered 98 feet above the deck and her mizzen stood 84 feet tall. Her sail area was about 4000 square feet. The yacht was built in 1949 in Denmark and was named in memory of her builder, Mr. Ring Andersen, who died shortly after the vessel was launched. The boat had been his pride and joy and the building had been under his constant supervision. A captain of one of the Norwegian cruise ships once visited us and explained that although working for a Norwegian Company, he was born in Denmark and had grown up in the vicinity of the Ring Andersen Shipyard. The yard had been his favourite playground and he clearly remembered the building of the *Ring Andersen*. He related to me how Mr. Ring Andersen, at age eighty-four, regardless of a stroke he had suffered and being restricted to a wheel chair, insisted on having himself lowered into the bilges of the vessel every day, for an inspection of the work in progress.

At around 9:00 A.M. the next morning we were hove to at Scarborough, Capital of Tobago, waiting for customs and immigration to clear us. Scarborough is on the east side of the Island. The resort is situated on the west side in Mount Irvine Bay, which gave the resort its name. After the formalities were over, we got underway again, rounded the Southern tip of the Island once more, staying well clear of Buccoo reef and proceeded to the bay which was to be our port for the next ten days. However, instead of anchoring, we poked our nose in and then went out again. Now came the task of updating the chart and exploring the West Coast of the island so that we could make some plans for our future daily trips. Armed with the ancient chart, hand bearing compass, parallel rulers and dividers, I busied myself taking bearings, making notes, checking depths and marking the findings on the old chart. I felt a bit like a modern day Captain Cook, except that I had more information to start with. He had nothing, which made his job slightly more difficult to say the least.

By late afternoon we had enough information to formulate a plan that would be appealing to our passengers. Armed with our newly found knowledge and up-dated chart, we returned to Mount Irvine Bay and this time dropped the hook to spend the night.

After dinner, David and I went ashore to the hotel to seek out the person in charge. It didn't take long to find him. He had been awaiting our arrival, anxiously, and had become quite alarmed when, earlier in the day, we had entered the bay and then left again. Our return was welcomed with much relief. The gentleman turned out to be the insurance company's vice president. He was a very pleasant individual and immediately agreed to our proposed curriculum. Passengers were to board at ten o'clock. We would sail them up the coast to a secluded bay, where, those interested, could swim or snorkel on an adjacent reef. Then, lunch would be served and we would sail back to Mount Irvine Bay. We were to return at about five o'clock.

The next morning our guests started to arrive. We picked them up from the shore in our tenders and ferried them on board. There were only some twenty candidates for the day's sail. When we returned later that day, the group had such a good time that they were reluctant to leave. The last passengers left the ship long after we had anchored.

The good news about the *Ring Andersen* spread, because the next morning at least 40 eager customers were waiting on shore. After that, we had to limit the numbers, as the contingent rapidly became larger each day.

One rule we had instigated was that all passengers removed footwear when boarding. "No shoes allowed on board, please!" we announced, as people arrived at the gangway. This was turned into a joke by the vice president. When, at the conclusion of the convention, we were invited to a gala ball, we found him dressed in an immaculate tuxedo with bow tie, and bare feet!

As the drinks were being served on board, Aubrey, our steward who had set up a bar, kept track of the number of drinks served by keeping a tab. At the end of each day David added up the check marks on the tab, and since each drink cost one dollar, there was no complicated arithmetic to perform. When the ten days had come to an end, David gave me the total for the lunches and the drinks. I looked at the account and did a double take when I noticed the amount of drinks consumed; 4232.

"What!" I exclaimed," That's—that's—Holy cow!"

"Yes," said David, "I've checked it several times and it's absolutely correct."

"Jeez Dave, when I give this to them, they'll think that we're trying to pull a fast one!"

"I know," replied Dave. "But it is correct, let's face it, these people drank a lot. It started with Bloody Marys in the morning, then onto the rum punch, it never let up. Quite often they didn't get off the boat until nine o'clock in the evening. They know the booze is free, the company is paying for it! The amazing thing is that we haven't had any drunks on board. Some were a bit happy perhaps, but no drunks."

"True," I mused,"but how do we break the news to Mr. Vice President?"

I asked Dave for all the chits and his work sheets. I put these together with the final bill into a large envelope and trotted off for a pow-wow with the big chief. When I found him, I made sure that he was seated comfortably in a big leather settee.

"Ahemm," I began,"I have a slight problem here."

"Oh?," he said, looking at me questioningly, "What is it?"

"Well, you see, about this bill. The liquor part of it. It's a bit higher than you'd probably expect."

The man looked concerned. A frown creased his forehead.

"See," I told myself, the man's already

upset. You have blown it. The first charter with *Ring Andersen* and he thinks you're a crook, trying to hold him up with a padded bill. "Go on," he urged,"how much is it?"

"Four thousand and two hundred and thirty two dollars," I blurted out and then hastened to add,"I have all the chits here, you can check, it's really accurate. Aubrey kept a record, he has no reason to cheat."

I watched the vice president's face and to my astonishment he started to shake with laughter. The tears rolled down his cheeks while he grabbed me by the hand and pulled me down into the chair beside him.

"Sit down my friend," he chuckled. He pulled a hand-kerchief from his pocket to wipe the tears from his face. "Let me explain a few things to you about our conventions. We hold these affairs annually. Each time they're held in a different area. I don't remember the exact expense figures for each year, but I do remember the amount of the bar bill of our previous convention which was held in Paris. Do you know what the bar bill for the hotel came to?"

He looked at me, to watch my reaction. I shook my head.

He slapped my knee with each syllable, annunciating each word,"Thirty two thousand dollars!"

I just about fell out of the chair. Without a further word I handed him the bill.

After the charter we spent a day touring the island, then weighed anchor in the evening and arrived back in Grenada in the early hours of the next day.

Anchored at the Tobago Keys.

The Aft Deck

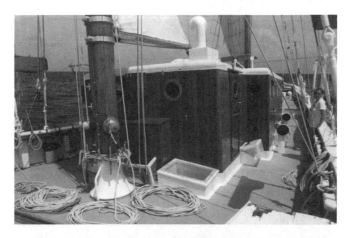

On deck, looking aft

The main saloon - dining room

The Clientele

The Tobago charter was behind us, many charters ago. Since that time, the nautical miles have steadily slipped away under *Ring's* keel. We were in the luxury end of the business, and for this the *Ring Andersen* was highly suited. The interior accommodation was such that we could offer three couples almost equal accommodation in separate staterooms. Each stateroom was larger than those of most ocean liners and included comfortable berths, an en-suite bathroom, a seating area, a writing desk, and other amenities of comfort. The ship boasted a separate library with sofas, chairs, a desk, and some four thousand books. The dining room and general sitting room were located on deck in what in nautical terms is called the deck house. Equipped with large port holes it provided a good view of the outside scenery. All interior walls and cabinets were made of luxuriously varnished Honduras mahogany. The deck house and the railings were made of teak. The aft deck had a teak wood raised section which provided seating for a dozen or so, or it could be used for sun bathing. All teak wood was varnished to a high gloss and as smooth as a polished grandfather clock. Other yachtsmen who knew how much work was involved in keeping a varnished surface in good condition would look in awe at the *Ring Andersen's* expanse of bright work and exclaim,"Holy smokes! There are acres of varnish there."

One of the features of chartering is the opportunity to meet people one would otherwise seldom encounter. What makes chartering unique is the fact that the charter operator will be living with his clientele in a relatively confined space for the entire charter term. Thus, the contact between the operator, I prefer to call him the host, and the customer, to whom I refer as the guest, is much closer than that in any other type of business. Obviously, here lies a rare opportunity to get to know one another very well, including all the idiosyncrasies the individuals might possess.

Most charters are booked through charter brokers. These people are professionals who arrange charters in return for a commission. A good charter broker will know the boat and the crew and captain personally. The broker is aware of the close contact of long duration between host and guests. The first rate broker will match the boat, guests and host. This of course takes a lot of know-how and experience, and it can mean the difference between a good and a bad charter. We have been very fortunate in this respect, since I do not recall having had a bad charter. We have, however, had some that were less interesting, or took a lot more work and effort than others, but on the whole, the vast majority have turned out to be extremely enjoyable.

I for one will admit to having met people I would never have met had it not been for chartering. We have catered to famous movie stars, highly placed government officials, and some very, very rich people. One such movie star turned out to be a bit of a pain, since he insisted on having the crew take him out in the middle of the night to go for a swim far away from shore. Much to his disappointment, I refused to accommodate him in this escapade, since for one, my crew earned their nightly rest; and further more, I did not fancy carrying his remains back to port after a run-in with a shark.

Had it not been for chartering, we would have never met people such as Robert De Niro, who regardless of his fame turned out to be a very likeable and level-headed person. Had it not been for chartering, I would never have met William Styron, the author. It was during a charter on board the *Ring Andersen* when he received the news that his novel, *Sophie's Choice*, was to be published by the Double Day Book Club. We had the privilege of reading the chapters of the manuscript, as they were passed around onboard, while he was putting on the finishing touches. It was Mr. Styron who encouraged me to write and to some extent, he is responsible for this book, *No Shoes Allowed*. When one evening, while relaxing on *Ring's* comfortable aft deck seating area, I confessed my secret ambition to him, he said, "You have the talent to tell (talk) a good story. All it takes now is to put it on paper. Just do it and you'll be alright."

After a while, one becomes rather blasé about the various dignitaries encountered in the charter circuit. A funny encounter took place at one time on the docks of Grenada Yacht Services.

Paul Newman and party had chartered the

yacht *Circe*. The yacht was tied up at the dock in the marina, and Mr. Newman and a friend were stretching their legs on the dock. They walked back and forth, deep in conversation. Except for an occasional greeting or smile of recognition, Mr. Newman and friend were left to their own devices. The only person somewhat baffled by the famous actor's appearance was Don Hack. Don was the owner of a craft called the *Rumrunner*. He took tourists out for short excursions to a nearby reef where they could snorkel or drink the rum punch that was served in liberal quantities. Don was doing some maintenance on his vessel and had observed the celebrity walk past him as he and his friend promenaded up and down the dock. Don had probably seen Mr. Newman on the screen countless different times, but for some reason he could not put a name to the familiar face. This frustrated Don to no end. Up and down the dock the movie star walked, back and forth, back and forth. Each time he passed the *Rumrunner* Don peered at him, trying to put a name to the well known face. Suddenly it came to him. "*Of course*," he thought, "*how could I have been so stupid?*" He was so happy with his recollection that for some reason he felt he should share it with the famous star. Just then, the twosome was again approaching the vicinity of the *Rumrunner*. Don rushed toward the couple and confronted them. With a voice resolute and bubbling with excitement, he victoriously exclaimed to Mr. Newman;

"I know who you are!"

The response drew raised eye brows and an amused look from the pedestrian.

"You're Marlon Brando!" cried Don triumphantly.

The wealthiest guests were the ones I found the most congenial on board. They were past the stage of finding the need to impress people with their importance. They seldom talked about their fortunes and were usually the least demanding. They appreciated everything that came their way and treated my crew with the respect they deserved. The odd time there might be one in the crowd who was an exception to the rule.

Once we had a lady on board who for some reason was intimidated by the rather posh, British accent of my purser and wife, Julian, known to her friends as Jules. The lady guest quickly adopted a highly exaggerated British accent herself and frequently stunned Jules by coming out with the most peculiar questions. Quite frankly, I believe the lady was a bit dim, if you get my drift, and more liberally endowed with money than with brains. One evening when we were seated at the dining table and the steward brought in a beautifully decorated duck a l'orange, she turned to Jules and said in her phony accent,

"I say, where was this duck shot?"

To which Jules responded,

"It comes from Hubbards, actually," referring to the food store where we did most of our provisioning.

"How exciting!" The lady commented, apparently assuming Hubbards was some large hunting estate in Grenada.

"Do you hunt there often?"

With a desperate look thrown in my direction,

Jules replied, "Yes, prior to each charter." Then she quickly excused herself from the table to check on some imaginary task in the galley, leaving it to me to diplomatically change the topic of conversation.

It is amazing how incredibly rich some people are. I always thought that being wealthy meant having a couple of million bucks stashed away in an old sock. I have learned since then that this is merely chicken feed. A long time ago I had ambitions of becoming rich. It is a good thing I abandoned that idea, because in relation to the really wealthy I would have been a failure. Instead, I have been successful in maintaining my struggle for the level of average.

One charter party we had on board consisted of a middle aged lady, her two daughters, their two children, and a gentleman. The gentleman was the lady's accountant and business advisor. He had been instructed to go along on the trip mainly to act as an escort and chaperon, and possibly to be near at hand in case an urgent business matter should come up. One evening I was having a night cap with the man in the lounging area on the aft deck. The rest of the party had retired for the night. The accountant let me in on some of the mysteries of high finance. He explained to me for instance, that his employer, in order to reduce her taxable income, gave away to each of her children and grandchildren, one million dollars every year. This apparently is the maximum amount one is allowed to pass on to one's heirs without it becoming taxable. From this information I deduced that the grandchildren had to be worth twelve million each, and the two daughters somewhere around thirty five million, give or take a few bucks here and there.

On another occasion, my daughter Michele and I visited with charter guests in the U.S. The two couples, who had been guests on the *Ring Andersen* repeatedly, sometimes twice a year and usually for three weeks at a time, had heard of our forthcoming trip to Vancouver. They insisted that we spend a few days with them since we would be travelling through their place of domicile. We had finished dinner at the indescribable home of one of the couples. All six of us retired to the library to continue our chat in a U shaped seating area. The two gentlemen sat to the right of me on a settee, while I was seated in a comfortable arm chair. Michele sat to my left in another chair, and she was engaged in a conversation with the two ladies who were seated in another settee to her left. While the three ladies were involved in discussing a topic of their interest, the subject of us men was foreign exchange. The American dollar had taken quite a beating, especially in relation to the Swiss franc. Foreign exchange was of great interest to me. When chartering to an international clientele, we had to deal with foreign currency frequently. Suddenly, one of the ladies asked me a question which drew me into their conversation. I answered politely, but my interest was still held by the male topic. While speaking with the ladies, I automatically kept one ear open to the subject being discussed by the men. I heard the following dialogue:

"You know, John, I'm really hurting."

"Yes, Charlie, I've heard you say that before,

but how much did you actually lose?"

I couldn't help but sharpen my ears. I heard Charlie reply,

"Twenty three million."

John whistled through his teeth and said,"Holy smokes! That's a lot of money."

There was silence for a while before John continued and said, consoling his friend,

"But let's face it, Charlie, losing twenty three million won't alter your lifestyle."

Grudgingly Charlie muttered in reply,

"No, I suppose not, but it's still a whole lot of money."

When a few days later Michele and I continued our flight, I wondered what it would be like dealing with such sums on the foreign exchange market. Furthermore, if that was the amount lost because of a partial drop of the dollar, what was the amount of the principal? I tried to imagine that kind of money, but I couldn't.

My favourite charter guests are Americans. I like Americans anyway. They have imagination and guts. The U.S. is one of the few places where an idea is still worth something. When they go for it, they do it in style. When the Americans build a marina, by gosh, they don't fool around. Beautiful docks, electric power, telephones, paved parking, cable TV, showers, and everything else you could wish for. They are also very much aware of the fact that the sea is not a place for dumping garbage, which is more than I can say for a lot of the French yachtsmen I have encountered. For a while it got so bad in the Islands that the government of St. Vincent had to post 'Do not dump garbage' signs on the beaches of Bequia. Bequia is a small Island governed by St. Vincent. Even though the official language is English, the signs were written in French. This I find remarkable, since the famous Frenchman, Mr. Cousteau, has done so much to make the world aware of the pollution problem.

Maybe it is because of the language barrier, but most French charters are difficult and more trouble than they are worth. In November of 1973, we started a charter with three French couples. As soon as they arrived on board I knew this group was going to be a challenge. As they stepped through the boarding gate, they brushed past me without introductions and ordered the crew to sort out their luggage without further ado. I might be regarded as slightly old fashioned where certain traditions are concerned, but I believe in proper introductions when boarding, especially when one expects to spend three weeks together. I also took a certain amount of pride in being the *Ring Andersen's* captain, and as I thought that it was my job to give orders to my crew and not theirs, I felt as if I had been demoted from my position. With hurt pride I let the invaders take possession of the ship. Giving them the benefit of the doubt, I hoped that their dictatorial behaviour was due to a tiring flight from France. Perhaps they would mellow once they had settled down in their new surroundings.

One hour later the party was comfortably seated with the customary rum punch in the deck chairs on the aft deck. Usually at this time

I introduce the guests to the rules of shipboard life. I asked for their attention and began rattling off the do's and don'ts: No shoes on board, please; close all doors or leave them in their fully open position, securely latched to the gadgets provided; do not waste water; turn off the lights and flush the toilets thoroughly; and make sure that everything that goes into the toilet has passed through your stomach first. Then I asked if they had anything in particular they were interested in, such as water skiing, swimming, sight seeing, snorkelling, and so forth. The last question enabled me to decide on an itinerary that would be enjoyable to everyone. Having come to the end of my speech, I pulled up a chair, sat down, and watched. The group's age, I guessed, varied from about forty to fifty years. They were good-looking people, the men appearing well groomed and prosperous. The ladies wore expensive jewellery and were dressed in fashionable garments. My French being rusty, I had addressed the group in English. Judging by the way they had ordered the crew around, they were obviously more at home with the English language than I was with French.

As I was sizing up my newly acquired clientele, they cast wary glances at me. I don't think they had expected a person on board who would tell them what they could and could not do. A rapid interchange of French conversation erupted. Everybody was speaking at once. It sounded like machine gun fire; much too fast for me to understand. In the meantime, I concentrated on guessing who was whom. The charter contract had listed the names of the guests.

I assumed the big fellow with the full head of grey hair to be Monsieur Pierre Valin, organiser of the charter party. He was the calmest of the group, occasionally answering a question or making a remark to which the others listened with attention. Presumably, the skinny lady with the straight black hair was his wife. At least, she made the most noise and appeared to be more demanding towards Monsieur Valin than any of the others. It turned out I was right.

The crowd quieted down, interrupted by suggestions and questions from madame. The gray haired gent scraped his throat, turned towards me and began to speak.

"Hm, hm, Captain, ve vant to do all ze zings you mentioned—"

Madame interrupted,"Tatatatatatata."

"Ah oui, ze men will dive wiz ze scuba and spearfish."

This sounded like a reasonable request, but I had reservations about the spear fishing. I had seen too many burly fishermen spear beautiful, tiny reef fish just for the sport of shooting them, only to discard them, mutilated, back into the water. We discussed an itinerary which would suit the desired activities, and after this was done, I mentioned that it would be nice if Monsieur Valin— "You are Monsieur Valin, aren't you?" —would introduce his friends. He hastened to introduce his party. Having done this part of my job, I excused myself and departed to advise the crew that we would be getting underway.

That evening we sat down for a pleasant but noisy meal. The afternoon's sail to a nice, calm anchorage had mellowed the attitudes considerably. I think that they had even started to accept me into their midst, somewhat reluctantly perhaps, but they had resigned themselves to the fact that there was only going to be one captain on this cruise. I was sitting in my usual seat which was at the head of one end of the long dining room table. Monsieur Valin sat at the other end, and the other guests were seated along both sides. Madame Valin was seated next to me on one side of the table, which was unlucky, because she had the habit of speaking with a full mouth, thus occasionally spraying my face whenever she spoke to me. Fortunately, she was usually addressing someone at the far end of the table. She spoke with a loud voice, as did her friends, in order to be heard over the other conversations going on at the same time. Although the noise level was extraordinary, I was quite happy that Madame's face was turned away from me most of the time.

"Captain, what nationality are the majority of your clientele?" Monsieur Valin asked from across the table. The others fell silent to listen to my reply.

"Mostly Americans," I answered.

"They must be very—what is the word—unpleasant?" one of the ladies suggested, wrinkling her nose with disapproval.

"No," I replied, turning to her. "Why do you say that?"

"Well, don't they drink a lot, and aren't they very demanding?"

"Yes," I said,"they do drink quite a bit, I suppose, but no, they are not demanding. In fact," I added,"they are very good charter guests."

For a while, as they thought about my answer, it was quiet around the table.

"But if they are drunk all the time, aren't they rather—"

"Uncouth?" I suggested.

"Yes, uncouth, that is what I mean."

"No, they are not uncouth," I replied. "Besides, I never said that they were drunk. They do drink a lot, but never to the point that they aren't courteous and considerate to others."

For the next several days this type of dialogue was repeated over and over again. They seemed determined to impress the picture of the ugly American upon me. They were constantly fishing for an opening to get me to agree that Americans are not as sophisticated, polished, well mannered, and civilised as the French. I wasn't having any of it, and politely but firmly rebutted the questioning.

These people were more nationalistic than the Germans during the second world war. Everything that was French was the best. They knew more about scuba diving than anybody; after all, Jacques Cousteau is French, is he not? Every Frenchman they met on shore was un amie and knew more about good places to visit than anyone else. This eventually became a problem, because I am sure that they felt that I, not being French and obviously an American sympathiser, was not to be trusted. On several occasions they arrived on board just having met a brother Frenchie and announced that they wanted to go to such and such a place, because it had been recommended by their pal on shore. In most instances the places were highly unsuitable for anchoring, and I had to say no to their requests. The people they talked with on shore were tourists and did not know the area well enough to be able to judge whether the recommended places were really worth visiting, let alone if they were accessible by a boat the size of the *Ring Andersen*.

"Yes, vell," he said "zere vas a boat anchored in zere."

"How big a boat? What kind of a boat, a dinghy?"

"He did not say, but it must be big because zere vere many people in it."

"Okay, let me show you on the chart. See? Those are not metres, they're feet. Here it shows, three feet! The boat your friend saw was a dinghy, a Boston Whaler perhaps. If you definitely want to go there we'll take you in our Boston Whaler, but not in the *Ring Andersen*. Besides, I know the place; it is nice for those poor sods on shore who have no boat to take them to better places. But it is nothing compared to the anchorages you have already visited with the *Ring*, believe me!"

But they did not believe me. They were quite sure that their foreign skipper was out to short change them. After a while, I became tired of arguing with them, and when once again they returned from a shore expedition with first hand information about a place magnifique, I let them have their way. The spot they had heard of was in the middle of nowhere, about forty miles out into the open Caribbean. Except for a couple of rocky outcrops the size of a postage stamp, the anchorage was unprotected and open to the unruly Caribbean swell. The place was sometimes visited by commercial spear fishermen with fast speed boats. They would go in, shoot their prey, and then get out as fast as possible. I explained all this to my guests, but added that if they still wanted to go, I would take them. One condition though, the distance involved would not allow us to get there and back in daylight, so once there, even if their French friend had been wrong, we would have to stay for the night. It was a foregone conclusion. Presumably, they had not believed a word I had said about the rough anchorage. Their friend had recommended the place, so it had to be magnificent.

Off we went with an early start the next morning. As usual, there was a stiff wind blowing. At about eleven o'clock I could see two little pinnacles sticking out from the sea. I picked up the binoculars and studied our new cruising domain as it loomed before us. Big waves were crashing over the rocks. The bald rock surfaces, wet from the breakers, shimmered in the bright sunlight. Not even a seagull was to be seen near this desolate place. Before long, the area became visible to the charter guests. With awe they viewed the spectacle growing more forbidding as we drew closer.

We anchored in good, sandy, holding ground, behind one of the rocks. The water boiled around us as the equatorial current swirled around the tiny islets. The yacht rolled behind her anchor like a drunken hippopotamus. I went to the foredeck to have a chat with my crew.

"Who wants to volunteer to take a few people for a wild ride?" I asked.

"What's up, Skip?"

"We're going to take our guests for a little fishing trip."

"Out here? You kidding, Skip?"

"No, I'm not!"

The crew were all familiar with the difficulties I had been experiencing with the French group. I explained to them that having gone through all the trouble of coming to this forsaken spot, I now wanted to prove a point and take them out in one of the Boston Whalers to the area where the spear fishing was to take place. I was sure they would not be out for long. In fact, I was quite certain they would not dare leave the dinghy, so it would only mean a quick ride through the turbulent seas. As I had expected, Thomas was eager to give it a go. Displaying a big grin on his face, he declared that he would give them the ride of their lives. I walked back to the passengers and told them that the dinghy would soon be ready to take the fishermen to the hunting grounds. I noticed that the group was somewhat subdued.

Launching the Whaler was not easy. The *Ring* was rolling violently, and it was quite a task to prevent the dinghy from bashing the hull. Once in the water, it was hauled out on the boat-boom and rode the waves at a safe distance. We were now ready for the expedition. I turned to the passengers and cheerfully announced that the boat was launched and ready for their departure. There was no response. The aft deck reminded me a little of a battle field. The chairs were folded up and put flat on their backs. Sitting in them was unsafe with the rolling motion of the ship.

The French army was scattered amongst the deck cushions, most of them in the horizontal position, and some of them holding on to the railing, steadying themselves against the heaving motion. I detected some greenish looking faces. Conversation was hushed and sporadic. I switched on the depth sounder and checked the reading. The instrument was not working properly. "*Probably because of poor contact with the transducer cable,*" I thought. I pulled the plug out of its socket and with a knife started scraping the contacts. I was within earshot of the little group. They were now talking slowly. I could follow the conversation.

"Why did he take us here?" Madame Valin mumbled.

"Because we asked him," came the reply from one of the men.

"Because we asked him? You mean because you asked him. I don't want to go spear fishing. He told you this place was no good for anchoring, didn't he?"

"Yes, but François —"

"François, François, François," she interrupted. "Who is this François anyhow? Some bum you met on the beach? What does he know, eh? Eh?"

"No use arguing about it," Monsieur Valin remarked,"we are here now, so let's make the most of it."

"Make the most of it? You are not going in that little boat. I won't hear of it. What do you want to do, commit suicide? Further more, we are stuck here. Don't you remember what he said? We have to spend the night here because it's too dangerous to sail amongst the reefs in the dark."

Total silence encompassed the group. As I fiddled with the depth sounder, I thought about the conversation I had overheard. They were actually not such a bad bunch. In spite of their particular idiosyncrasies, we had been able to get along pretty well. They just did not know any better. It was my job to give the charter guests a good time. After all, that's what they paid for. They were certainly not happy now. I figured I had better do something about it. I plugged in the transducer cable and checked the monitor. It was working fine. I switched the set off and turned to the guests.

"Look," I said, "I am sorry that this place has turned out to be such a disappointment. Obviously, you don't want to go out diving in this current and in these seas. I can't blame you, and I would prefer if you didn't anyway. Only professional divers fish here, and even for them it is a tough spot. I know that I said that we must stay here for the night, but if we leave right now we can go to St. Barts, which is a good harbour with a good lighthouse. I don't mind going in there at night. What do you say?"

I didn't have to ask the last question. I had seen the faces cheer up while making my little speech. In no time the dinghy was hoisted back into the davits, this time helped by eager hands from the male passengers. The whole exercise was cheered on by the ladies. I was amazed at the change that had taken place as I watched the guests pull with all their might, side by side with the crew. Soon the anchor was secured on board and we were on our way, the sails settling us on a comfortable tack to our destination. That evening, as we sailed into the sunset, we saw the green flash for the first time that trip. This phenomenon takes place the very second the sun disappears behind the horizon. For a fraction of time, the sky lights up with a bright luminous green aura. It is quite a spectacle to watch. To the experienced observer, it can be seen several times by crouching low on the deck and then quickly standing up the very instant the green flash appears. We slipped into St. Barts late that night.

The next day was spent at anchor in the harbour. St. Barts is a department of France and it is a duty free port. It is the hub of the Caribbean smuggling fraternity. Island schooners could be seen taking aboard illicit cargoes of cigarettes and liquor. The island had a small population which survives to a large extent on tourism and the sales of wares to the smugglers. The island also features one of the best ship chandleries in the Caribbean. The store did a thriving business in the sales of outboard motors, inflatable and fibreglass dinghies, stainless steel hardware and cordage, plus other numerous items needed on sea going vessels.

The guests were on shore seeing the sights. I had taken the opportunity to do some reading. I was in my cabin, bent over a book when I heard a commotion on deck. I looked at my watch. It was almost six o'clock. "Must be the guests," I muttered, speaking to myself. "It is getting close to dinner time." I kept on reading. After about ten minutes I put the book down again and listened. I could hear dinghies coming and going, accompanied by footsteps on deck.

It sounded like many footsteps, certainly more than six passengers would produce. I put the book down and stood up to investigate. When I arrived on deck, I spotted several people milling around. Some I recognised as our guests, but the others I had never seen before. The total was about twenty fast speaking Frenchmen. I mingled in amongst the group, assuming that one of our guests would enlighten me with some kind of explanation. As I bumped from person to person, some activity caught my eye. There appeared to be a lot of dinghies around, several of which were occupied by people dressed in party clothes. In fact, they were dressed in similar attire as the party occupying the *Ring's* aft deck. I also noticed that the dinghies were headed in our direction, one of them approaching the gangway that very moment.

"Well, I'll be," I thought. "They have done it again."

I rushed to the gangway to intercept the approaching dinghy. I arrived just in time to see a lady clad in jewellery, cocktail dress, and shoes with high spiked heels, step onto the boarding ladder. Blocking the gate's entrance, I queried, "Can I help you?"

As if I had insulted her, she looked me up and down and said, "I am coming aboard."

"Not in those shoes, you aren't." And speaking to the fellow driving the dinghy, I added, "Wait a minute, friend, don't go away yet."

"What do you mean?" she said, obviously agitated. "What is wrong with my shoes, and who are you anyway?"

"This is my boat, madame, and I do not allow

shoes on board. They wreck my varnish. Certainly those," I said, pointing at her big spikes.

"Well, I don't care who you are. I am a friend of Madame and Monsieur Valin. This is their yacht; they have chartered it."

The lady was beginning to anger me, and as calmly as I could I countered her last words by saying,"You could not possibly be a friend of the Valins, because if you were, they would have notified me of your arrival. Furthermore, the Valins have chartered this yacht for a party of six, not for the entire population of France. So please, remove yourself from the gangway and get back into your dinghy."

I watched her step back into the skiff and take off in a huff. Just then, Twin, our chef, approached and said,"Skip, can I have a word with you?"

"Sure, Twin, what's the problem?" I asked, as I pulled him into the chartroom, away from the crowd.

"Dinner is going to be a little late, Skip. I won't be able to have it ready on time."

"Why not? Have we run out of cooking gas?"

"No, we're okay for gas, but the lady told me that we would be having extra guests for dinner, and—"

"Which lady," I interrupted. "You mean Madame Valin?"

"Yes, Skip."

"Listen, Twin, you just get dinner ready on time for the usual amount of people. Pay no attention to what anyone else tells you, understand?"

Twin marched off. This time they had gone too far. Determined to get a few things straightened out, I went in search of the Valins. I did not have to go far. As I was about to step onto the deck, I bumped into Monsieur Valin.

"Ah, Captain," he said. "I have been looking for you. My wife told me that you sent one of her friends away and told her that she was not allowed on board."

"You're damn right!" I lit into him. "And I have been meaning to have a little talk with you. Every day during dinner we have had little chats about the behaviour of Americans. Every time you've tried to suggest to me that they don't know how to behave, that they are drunks and that they are inferior to the sophisticated French. Well, let me tell you this: Americans have always had the courtesy to introduce their guests. Not only that, they have also always been considerate enough to ask if it was okay to invite friends on board. After all, I own this boat; you have not bought it, you have chartered it. If you have read the charter contract, you must know that the number and names of the party are listed in the agreement. In any event, it does not include all these people who, I am certain, you don't really know any better than I do. Another thing is that you should know better than to pass out orders to my cook without consulting me first. Anyhow, nobody gives orders to my crew except me. Now, Monsieur Valin, would you be so good as to advise your friends from shore to remove themselves from my ship so that we can have dinner without further disturbances, Please!"

I was livid, and Monsieur Valin could tell. Without saying a word he departed, and after a few minutes the invasion began to leave the ship.

Half an hour later we sat in our usual places at the table. Nobody said a word. All that could be heard was the sound of the cutlery on the dishes. The stereo was playing softly, and the candles spread a cosy glow of warm light on the varnished woodwork of the saloon. Rightly or wrongly, and since I had already made my feelings known to Monsieur Valin, I could not resist digging the knife in a bit deeper. I sat back in my chair, looked around the subdued table and said,

"Well, isn't this nice. Finally we're enjoying a civilised dinner. Nobody's screaming their lungs out; we can even hear the music playing in the background. As a matter of fact, this is just like an American charter!"

The silence prevailed until Monsieur Valin put his fork and knife down and said,

"Captain, I have thought about what you said to me earlier and we owe you an apology. You were quite right in making me aware of our habit of constantly criticising the American way of living. We have obviously been so busy pointing the finger at others that we have lost complete evaluation of ourselves. I am afraid that in doing so we labelled ourselves the Ugly French. Please accept our apologies."

I was impressed. It requires character to make an apology like that. Now that the air had been cleared, the tension subsided. Ten minutes later the guests were back to their usual shouting match, and I kept well out of range of Madame Valin to avoid being sprayed. But then, you can't win them all, can you?

The Trespasser

One of the first things I did when I took over the *Ring Andersen* was to get rid of her anchors. The yacht carried two Navy anchors through hawse pipes on her bows.

I don't care much for Navy anchors. Their only contribution to holding a ship in place comes from their sheer bulk and weight alone. To make them effective, one has to dump miles of chain on them, but then still, in a good blow, I feel uneasy. The *Ring Andersen's* navy anchors weighed 450 pounds each. I shuddered at the thought of having to crank them up by hand if ever something were to go wrong with the power of the anchor windlass.

I replaced both anchors with much lighter C.Q.R. anchors. In addition to the weight advantage, this type of anchor also folds quite nicely against the hull, and as the yacht strains against the wind in an open roadstead, the C.Q.R. digs deeper and deeper into the bottom.

One of the cumbersome Navies I sold to a small freighter named *Olga*. The *Olga* was typical of the type of freighter of which several ply the waters of the West Indies. Most of them are of Dutch origin and usually in the range of 250 tonnes. Another such type of vessel was owned by a friend of mine by the name of Peter Davies.

Peter is British, and one might say very British with the appropriate plummy accent. Peter had a red beard, very properly trimmed. He wears gold rimmed glasses and a constant serious expression on his face.

One of the problems when talking with Peter is that when he says anything funny one doesn't know if it is meant to be funny. Consequently, one doesn't know whether to laugh or to try and keep a straight face. This can cause great discomfort to the facial muscles of his audience.

Peter's ship is called *Hildur*. She was alongside the dock in Grenada waiting for a new load of cargo. Peter and I were standing on the dock watching a small freighter manoeuvre through the small channel leading to the lagoon in which Grenada Yacht Services is located. Presumably, she was coming into dock to undergo repairs. I suddenly recognised the freighter to be the *Olga*, the one which carried one of the *Ring's* old Navy anchors.

I said to Peter,"That's *Olga*. She has one of my old anchors."

Peter looked at me and asked,"Do you know *Olga's* Captain?"

"Not really," I replied,"I met him briefly when he bought that anchor. He was not very talkative, but," shrugging my shoulders, I added, "he seems quite a decent sort of guy."

"He's a disgusting fellow," Peter said with a smirk towards the freighter which had now come quite close."

Puzzled, I studied Peter's face and asked, "Oh, how so?"

"Well, I tell you, old chap, he's one of the most revolting individuals I've ever met." Agitated, he tugged at the whiskers of his well groomed beard and then proceeded to tell me his story.

"I was alongside the dock in Trinidad waiting to take on cargo. The harbour was full of ships, and dockage space was very limited. Several local schooners and island freighters were doubled up alongside the dock. "*Olga*," Peter gestured to the little freighter now coming up to the dock, "was tied up next to me on my starboard side. It was about four o'clock in the afternoon, and I was having a cup of tea on deck in front of my wheelhouse, when suddenly I saw — you know what I saw?" he interrupted, examining me sternly.

I shrugged my shoulders and said, "No, what did you see?"

Pointing towards *Olga*, Peter exploded,"I saw him! He was sitting on my starboard railing having a shit! Imagine! Him, having a shit off my railing, in broad daylight in front of me while I'm enjoying a cup of tea on my own ship!"

I visualized Peter sitting in his deckchair, saucer in his left hand, teacup neatly in the right, little finger pointing upwards, back straight and erect, making the discovery of *Olga*'s captain relaxing with his pants down and his rear end hanging over the side of Peter's ship.

I had great difficulty seeing the seriousness of the situation, and all I could stammer with a straight face was, "You — you're kidding."

"By George, I'm not. It's the truth," Peter exclaimed, and he glared at me expectantly.

Realizing there was more to come, I encouraged him, "Then what happened?"

"Well," Peter said, shaking his fist at *Olga*, "I yelled, Hey! You there, get off my ship this instant!" Peter stopped for a moment and then he whispered, "Do you know what that good for nothing did?"

Without waiting for my reply he continued, emphasizing each word separately, "He picked up the end of my brand new mooring line and wiped his rear end with it!"

Peter's eyes penetrated deeply into mine as he went on, again speaking slowly, making sure the seriousness of the situation would be fully understood, "I had to cut ten feet off my brand new mooring line and throw it in the drink!"

I was almost certain that I detected a little twinkle in Peter's eyes when he made this last statement, but it was probably the sunshine reflecting on his glasses. To be on the safe side, and with great effort, I strained to keep a straight face while faking a surprised gasp that sort of sounded like "You don't say?"

Peter sold *Hildur* shortly afterwards to Captain Belmar from Petit Martinique. Peter and his family moved back to England. Unfortunately, I have lost touch with him. He is a valued friend to have. He is one of those guys who stands by you when you're in real need, not just with talk, but with deeds. People like that are hard to find. In fact, I owe Peter one. He helped me out once when I was in deep trouble.

But that's another story.

Friday the Thirteenth

It was one of those situations where everything that could go wrong did go wrong; a typical case where one failure followed another. To top it all off, it was Friday the thirteenth. Being a sailor, I should have known better than to set sail on that day.

Ring Andersen had just undergone a refit. We had spent some four months in the yard overhauling, painting, varnishing, and going through the yacht from stem to stern. She had been hauled, scrubbed and painted; the sails were mended where needed, and the rigging was gone over with a fine toothed comb. Even the generators had been taken apart, inspected and tuned.

Finally, the ship was glistening and sparkling and ready to go again. We were to start a charter in Martinique. I planned to depart from Grenada at six a.m. on Friday the thirteenth so we would be in Martinique on Saturday to pick up the charter party. By Thursday afternoon the provisions started to come on board and the frozen goods were placed in the deep freeze.

By ten o'clock in the evening I discovered

that the deep freeze was not working properly because the cooling water pump had broken down. Repair was out of the question since the windings had burnt out. I tried locating another pump motor without success. The electrical system for the deep freeze was 220 volts AC. The yacht also had 110 volts DC, but I could not locate a 110 volt motor either. I did eventually manage to get hold of a 12 volt DC electric pump, but is was four o'clock in the morning before, by means of a complicated combination of resistors, the 110 volt system was reduced to 12 volts. Anyhow, by four a.m. the deep freeze was working again. By this time I was dead tired and decided to delay sailing so I could get some sleep.

We motored out of the harbour at about one o'clock that afternoon and headed toward Martinique. When we cleared the northern end of Grenada we hoisted the sails and started beating into a stiff breeze of 40 knots with rough seas. To make better time, we were motor sailing. We also had one of the generators running to charge the batteries which had not been charged properly while we were in the yard. Around five thirty P.M. we were west of Union Island, and I decided to come about on a port tack to make a landfall before total darkness set in. Just after we had completed the tack, Thomas, our engineer, made a check in the engine room. When he came out he looked at me with alarm and exclaimed,

"Skip, the engine is on fire!"

"What?"

"There's fire coming out of the engine, Skip!"

I made a dive for the engine room, which was accessible from the aft deck through a hatch located near the steering station.

I must pause here to describe the yacht's engine. It was a Volund built by Burmeister and Wain, a Danish machine that was huge in size and weight. It developed 300 BHP at 150 RPM and was started by means of compressed air. The engine was four cycle and charged its own air starting supply through a starting valve located in the top of the engine head. It had two of these valves. Number one starting valve had blown completely out, and with every stroke of that particular cylinder a jet of flames burst from the engine.

I stopped the engine and examined the hole. It appeared that only the valve had blown out of its seat. The seat itself was still in good nick. Since we carried spares on board, it would not take too much to make repairs. For the time being, however, I had to wait until the engine cooled off. Besides, I preferred a calmer stretch of water to make repairs.

I went back on deck to see how we were progressing. Without the engine's help we had slowed down, but we were still moving at a good clip. I decided that we would wait with the repairs until morning and daylight, or possibly until we were at anchor in Martinique. Thomas was still in the engine room tidying up and afterwards went into the generator room which is located directly behind the main engine room. Both rooms were connected through a small passageway. Thomas had decided to check on the generator which was purring away, recharging our depleted batteries.

It was getting dark, and I switched on our running lights. Thomas appeared on deck again and said,

"Skip, I don't think the valve is the only thing wrong with the engine."

"How so, Thomas?" I asked.

"Well," replied Thomas, "there's about a foot of water in the generator room."

"What?" I gasped. "That's impossible. That valve is not in any way connected to water."

I considered that perhaps the valve had blown out because something had gone wrong with the cooling water. But how could that flood the generator room?

Down again I went, and indeed the generator room was flooding. It took me some time to realize that this could definitely not be related to the previous incident. But the water was warm! Suddenly, I looked at the exhaust of the generator. Sure enough, the muffler, which was an aqua lift, had a hole in it and all the cooling water from the generator was being pumped into the generator room.

"Shut down generator one and start generator two."

"No luck!"

The water had sloshed around so much that the electrical components of the other generator were wet, and it would not start.

I went back on deck and considered our predicament. An account of the situation ran through my head:

"The main engine is out and will take at least four hours to repair. The generators are out, our batteries are down, so no lights, no engine repair. Also, it is dark. Our running lights will not last long without full batteries. Most of all, our electric bilge pumps are now out too!"

With difficulty in the strong wind, I lit up a cigarette and then tossed it into the sea when the spray extinguished it. My thoughts continued,

"We are in shipping lanes with no navigation lights, no engine, no pumps. We can rig an oil light maybe; we have a manual pump which should be adequate. But then, maybe it isn't. We are heading into pretty big seas. *Ring* is a big wooden ship. She works and therefore leaks in a seaway like this."

Normally, I would have headed out to open sea, but we still had a long way to go before we cleared the shipping lanes. I did not like it. All things considered, I decided to put in somewhere for repairs before things got worse. We were still headed for Union Island. Again my mind reasoned:

"On the west side of the island is a bay. With a bit of fancy maneuvering I might get in there and drop the hook. I must be careful of the reef that sticks out and hope we don't get headed by the wind, which is very unpredictable because of the high hills. It's worth a try."

Into the bay we went. There was a moon out and visibility was pretty good in between clouds. There! We were almost in, but the wind whipped around and we couldn't make it. Just enough momentum to jibe around and sail out. I could see the reef close to port as the ship slowly turned.

Outside again! Let's try again. Come about, port tack, into the bay, head her up toward the anchorage.

No good. Headed again! Jibe, skim by the reef and out again.

Once more I tried without success. My nerves could not cope with a fourth try. Back to the drawing board.

On the south side of Union is Frigate Island. Just off the island is a little lagoon in which we could anchor.

Down helm again, tack to starboard. On port tack again, heading towards the new destination. On the south side of Union Island we were becalmed. Our way carries us towards the anchorage, not enough speed, we can't make it. Fall off, pick up a little breeze, and we sail by it. No, we need an engine for that one. Forget it, we will go to the west side of Carriacou, another, bigger island just south of Union Island. There is no bay there, but the west side offers some protection from the wind although the seas can be rough. There is the odd sandy spot, shallow enough to get the hook to dig in. Must be careful, though, also here the winds are fluky. We must get those sails down all at once and at the right time.

I mustered the entire crew.

"OK, fellows," I said, "this is what we'll do. When we hit the spot, I will blow the whistle and then I want all the sails to come down at the same time. Everybody take your stations. Mizzen, main, staysail, and jib all down in one crash. Anchor down at the second whistle, OK?"

All eight of us went into action. On a broad reach we sailed down the west coast of Carriacou. When we were just past our selected spot we downed helm and hardened up on the sails. We then pinched her and headed for the chosen place. The wind was still holding. She had to stop just in time, because we would be anchoring very close to the shore. We were doing fine.

Pinch a little more now. First whistle. All sails down! *Ring's* 220 tonnes of momentum slowly proceeded to her destination.

Oh, oh! Trouble. That sail is not coming down. The jib halyard is stuck. Everything is down except the jib. *Ring* has almost stopped. We are almost there!

"Get that jib down!"

"She won't come!"

The shrill sound of the second whistle rang across the deck.

"Anchor down!"

A plunge as the anchor hits the water. The chain rattles out. A gust of wind, from behind us! The jib billows out and catches the wind. *Ring Andersen* gains momentum. The anchor holds, but the chain still rattles out. The crew is applying the brake. Sparks are flying from the drum. At last, the chain is stopped off. Too late!

The boat had gone too far. The bow stopped, but the stern swung around and grounded on a small reef close to shore.

She was hard aground. As each swell passed underneath us, we could feel her pounding the rocky bottom under the keel. Just then, the fouled halyard was cleared away and the jib was lowered.

I quickly told the crew to launch one of the Boston Whalers to set a kedge anchor out to sea from the stern. Having done this, I made a dash for the chart room and turned the radio to 2182. It would be difficult to reach anyone at this time. I looked at my watch. It was nearly midnight. Radio stations in our vicinity would be closed down by now. The nearest help was at Petit St. Vincent, a small island with a luxury resort operated by Haze Richardson. He had a Striker of about 35 feet with powerful engines. The boat was used to take guests to and from the island.

"Mayday, Mayday, Mayday! This is the yacht *Ring Andersen*."

A moment's wait and then a faint crackled reply. I could not make it out.

Again,"Mayday, Mayday, Mayday! This is the yacht *Ring Andersen*."

This time I could identify the other station. It was the Coast Guard at Puerto Rico.

"Puerto Rico Coast Guard, this is the yacht *Ring Andersen*, Charlie Zulu three niner one niner. Do you read?"

The radio crackled again, but now there were other voices as well. I could not understand any of it.

Perhaps they hear me okay, I thought. I transmitted again. "My position is half a mile south of the north west point of Carriacou. Latitude—longitude—, please telephone Petit St. Vincent and advise them."

This time I heard Puerto Rico asking,

"Repeat your position."

I repeated and added, "Telephone Petit St. Vincent and advise them of our position."

Puerto Rico, barely audible, came back with, "Say again. You are breaking up. State number of passengers on board. Give a description of your vessel."

I clicked the transmitter button on the microphone and noticed that the light in the chart room had dimmed significantly. As I did so, I glanced at the instruments, and they confirmed that our batteries had almost petered out. I switched to the emergency power supply for the radio, but it also showed well below par. I threw the mike down and turned off the set. I was wasting my time here. Better go on deck and see if we can pry the ship loose.

The kedge anchor had been set and appeared to be holding. Even if we could get the yacht off the bottom and into deeper water, we would still need a tow to get us into a position with enough sea room to raise our sails.

I delegated two of the crew to take the Whaler to Petit St. Vincent to get help. It would be a rough ride for them. Petit St. Vincent was about 4 or 5 miles away, and even though there was some protection from the wind and seas due to some shelter offered by Union Island and a few small sandy islets, it was still quite a trip for an open boat, especially at night.

"Be careful," I said. "Take it easy and keep your speed down. No heroics out there."

"No problem, Skip." Aubrey and Thomas threw me a grin. "We will have *Striker* here soon. Don't worry about us."

My crew were excellent seamen and good boat handlers. A quick ride in the whaler with her 50 HP outboard engine was their favourite past time. This time I hoped they wouldn't try to break any speed records. Off they went into the night.

The moon had now disappeared. We were surrounded by almost total darkness. A few stars could be seen, but most of them were obscured by large clouds racing towards the south west. Except for the occasional williwaw that came down from the mountains of Carriacou, we were pretty well sheltered from the strong winds. These williwaws worried me, because as they swooped down the mountain and hit the water they curled back and pressed us closer to shore.

The remaining six of us were all heaving and pulling on the line that led to the kedge anchor. Each time a swell passed under us we pulled and made fast quickly. As the boat lifted on the next wave, it would put more strain on the anchor and move the ship away from shore. Bit by bit, little by little. At times it seemed that we made no progress at all. Sometimes I thought all our efforts were useless and *Ring Andersen* would pound herself to pieces right there. But still we heaved and pulled.

Suddenly, the pounding seemed to be less frequent. She was still touching, but not as hard as before. Hurray! We were winning. *Ring* was lying parallel to the shore, her bow pointing south. Our bow anchor was to starboard and slightly forward. The kedge was also to starboard, but slightly aft. If we now pulled alternately on the kedge and bow anchor, we might gradually wedge her off the bottom and get her into the clear. If we could only use the power winch it would be so much easier. With the rest of the crew still straining their backs on the kedge, I dove into the generator room and started to work on generator number two. This was the one that drove the windlass. I dried the electrical components as best I could, sent up a small prayer and pressed the button. Success! I looked at the dials: 220 volts AC right on the nose! No smell, no sparks. It's a good thing those generators had their own starting batteries. I quickly went back up on deck.

"Keep the pressure on that kedge, you guys. Raphael, you and I will work on the bow anchor."

The two of us went forward and started the windlass. Then we put pressure on the chain. The motor slowed down under the strain.

"Release her. Let's wait for the next swell."

We started the same technique we had applied to the kedge anchor. Carefully, little by little. We could not put too much pressure on. The windlass was very powerful, and if the ship would not come, we would run the risk of breaking the anchor out of its position. We could apply pressure only at short intervals.

At 4.40 a.m. the *Ring* was clear of the reef. She was now riding easy in enough water to keep her off the bottom. We were about 30 feet away from and parallel to the reef. We dared not haul her any further for fear of shifting the anchors. If one of them were to let go we would blow back onto the shore.

I had become worried about Aubrey and Thomas. Where was *Striker*? She should have been here by now. Why had the Whaler not come back yet?

I tried the radio once again. With the generator running, the batteries had regained some of their energy. I called Petit St. Vincent.

No reply. Suddenly; *"Ring Andersen*, this is *Striker*. We have Aubrey and Thomas on board and we are on our way."

I let out a sigh of relief. Some time later we saw the familiar shape of *Striker* appearing through the early light of dawn. Soon *Striker* was standing off within hailing distance. Haze Richardson's large frame loomed on the flying bridge.

"Wha' happen, Skip?" he yelled, turning on a West Indian accent.

"She run aground mon," I shouted back, picking up his manner. More seriously, I continued, "We pulled her off, but both our anchors are hove short. I don't want to disturb either of them until I get a line on you. Is that OK with you?"

"Ya, sure," replied Haze. "Throw us a line and we will keep you off while you break your anchors out. Then we had better tow you to the P.S.V. anchorage. You'll be safe there."

"Great," I hollered, "but won't our weight put too much strain on your equipment?"

"I don't think so," Haze yelled back. "We will do it slow and easy. Are you making any water?"

"Yes," I answered, "but it is not too bad. Our pumps appear to be able to handle it okay."

"Good," replied Haze. "Let's get cracking then."

In the mean time, Raphael had produced a heaving line and attached it to a hawser which could be used for towing. The monkey fist shot towards *Striker* where all hands pulled it in and secured the hawser to their vessel. Shortly thereafter, our anchors were secured on board and the procession got underway. We reached the anchorage at P.S.V. without further incident.

When we were safely anchored, Haze came on board with his friend Doug Terman. Haze and Doug used to operate a charter yacht called *Jacinta*. When they sold her they built the resort on the uninhabited island of Petit St. Vincent. Haze was still operating the resort, but Doug was no longer involved. Doug had bought a yacht and was cruising the islands.

I gave them the details of what had led to our near demise.

"Well," said Haze, as he gestured to Doug, "maybe we should call this anchorage Refuge Cove. Yesterday Doug, and now you."

I turned to Doug and asked, "What happened to you?"

"We lost our mast," answered Doug. "Snapped clear off the deck."

"Holy smokes," I said. "That'll be a real bugger finding a new mast in these parts.

Doug's yacht was a Trewes 48, a sturdy boat which had done a lot of travelling. Her name was *Encantada*.

"Yes," Doug said, "this weather is taking its toll. The yacht *Clover* struck a reef when they tried to enter the Blue Lagoon in St. Vincent. Fortunately, she is safe too. Made it with very little damage."

Later I was to learn that when I called the Mayday to the Puerto Rican Coast Guard, another Mayday was taking place. A British training ship had left Grenada bound for Trinidad. She had run into trouble somewhere along her route. Our messages were received at the same time by the Coast Guard and the positions got mixed up. The result was that neither of us were located during a search. What had become of the British ship was never reported to us. Confusion, confusion. Although our mishap was not caused by the weather, it had certainly made matters much more difficult.

Alas, there was a lesson to be learned. After a long refit, do some sea trials first to make sure that everything works properly. Most of all, never set sail on Friday the thirteenth. For God's sake, stay in port!

"You look tired," said Doug. "How about bacon and eggs on *Encantada* ?" Looking at his watch he commented, "Annie should have it ready just about now."

"Yes please," I replied.

After serving several cups of coffee, Doug, who has several novels to his credit, and his charming mate, Annie, explained why it had taken so long before *Striker* had come to the rescue. Apparently, when Thomas and Aubrey arrived on the island nobody knew where Haze was. Eventually the duo had started to systematically question every yacht in the harbour. When they arrived at the *Encantada* they hit bull's eye. When Haze and Doug heard of our need for help, they had *Striker* under way in less than fifteen minutes.

The rest of the day was spent assessing the damage and making repairs where possible. *Ring* was copper sheathed, and many of the plates were ripped or missing altogether. We had a fairly serious leak in the forepeak. There was damage all along the keel, and possibly the garboard strake had opened up. Part of the rudder shoe was broken off. Extensive repairs had to be made, and obviously this had to be done in the shipyard. *Ring* had to come out of the water and for this we had to go back to Grenada.

Arrangements had to be made for the charter party who were waiting for us to arrive in Martinique. I chartered a plane, so they could be flown to Grenada, where another yacht was standing by to take our place. We now come to the point of the story.

Towards late afternoon, Peter Davies arrived in the anchorage with *Hildur*. This came as a complete surprise to me. The anchorage of a luxury resort is not the place where one expects freighters to spend idle time. Before long, Peter came on board.

"I heard about your trouble. Tough luck."

"Yes, it's tough alright. Lost the charter too. It was a two weeker. Could have used the money after the refit. What brings you here?"

"I came to see if you needed help."

"You brought *Hildur* all the way up here to see if I needed help?"

"Yes. I figured that you would want to haul *Ring* out at the shipyard in Grenada, so I will escort you back down, in case you need assistance.

Later, in Grenada, the damage was assessed at somewhere in the vicinity of twenty thousand dollars. I discussed the terms of payment with the shipyard manager. I found myself in a dilemma. The yard would not start repairs without being paid in advance as the work progressed. The insurance company, on the other hand, would not pay until all the repairs were completed.

I could not advance the money because I did not have it. In fact, I was near broke. My spare cash had gone into *Ring's* lengthy refit, and the last of my funds had been spent on the charter flight for *Ring's* would-be guests. Peter, who had been within earshot of the somewhat heated discussions with the shipyard manager, suddenly interjected,

"Jan, can I have a word with you?"

I turned to Peter.

"Look," he continued,

"this isn't getting you anywhere. If you don't get your boat fixed soon, you will lose your other charters too. I have some money stashed away that I don't need at the moment. How about letting me advance you the twenty thousand until the insurance claim is settled?"

Due to Peter's generous offer, we were able to meet our next charter commitment.

Thanks, Peter, wherever you are!

Another Shitty Story

Close to the dry dock of Grenada Yacht Services is an area which is much frequented by the yachties from the charter boats. It is called the Patio Bar. It features chairs and tables scattered among the palm trees, a view of the marina and the dry dock, and best of all, tall drinks and roties! Roties are a popular West Indian delicacy. They resemble a rolled up version of a tortilla, stuffed with chicken, beef, or shrimp curry.

It was in this place where most of the problems of the world were solved. It was here, where during *Ring's* restoration, I relaxed or discussed the progress of the work. It was on one such occasion that several skippers from various charter yachts were gathered around a table. The table was well decked with the local favourites, Roties and Carib beer. Amongst the group was Peter Davies. I joined and grabbed a chair. The topic appeared to be that curse and evil of all charter skippers, The Head! That no good, below the waterline, valve-and-flopper-stop ridden piece of porcelain, the ship's toilet.

"Don't talk to me about head problems," I heard Peter say as I lowered myself into the chair. "I've had my fair share of them." He cast a glance around the table waiting for attention. He continued," Before I had *Hildur*, I was skipper of one of the windjammers, the *Yankee Clipper*, to be exact."

We all knew the *Yankee Clipper*. She was a large topsail schooner of about 140 feet. At one time she had been a beautiful private yacht before being converted to be able to take on a large number of passengers, somewhere around eighty, if my memory serves me right. She operated as a head boat, which means that people can book passage individually, rather than as a private group, which is the case with charter yachts. To make the fare economical and to be able to appeal to a larger market, a head boat generally fills up with as many bodies as possible. A charter yacht, on the other hand, rarely takes more than six guests. Needless to say, there is an appreciable difference in price. Compared to a charter yacht *Yankee Clipper* had to be rather crowded when fully booked.

I had some idea of the story Peter was leading up to. I had heard a tale about *Yankee Clipper's* heads rumoured along the grape vine, but I had no idea that Peter had been the ship's skipper. Was I now going to hear about it from the horse's mouth? I gave Peter my undivided attention.

"Yes," Peter continued when silence fell amongst the group, "the *Yankee's* heads were plugged—all of them. You see, they were all connected to a large holding tank. We had tried everything we could to find the blockage, but, no luck! It became quite a desperate situation because every berth in the ship was occupied. As you can imagine there were a lot of uncomfortable people on board, if you know what I mean!"

We all knew what he meant! Peter threw us a speculative glance over the top of his glasses. Appearing satisfied with our attention, he took a sip of his beer and continued, "The only avenue left unexplored was to try and tackle the problem in reverse. In other words, put pressure on the holding tank through the discharge pipe!"

With this comment, anticipation amongst Peter's audience increased substantially. We all looked at each other as Peter took another sip of Carib.

"I decided to give it a blast with the compressed air from a diving tank."

The implication of Peter's last statement hung in the air like a time bomb about to explode. Someone choked on a rotie. The audience had become very, very silent.

"Yes, well, I wasn't about to try this with all the passengers on board of course."

A sigh of relief from the listeners, or could I detect some disappointment?

"So, I sent all passengers ashore. Then, I went over the side with one of the crew and the diving bottle. I inserted the nozzle into the sewer outlet just above the waterline. I turned the valve and gave it a good blast, when suddenly I heard this horrendous scream! The sound appeared to have come from on deck. I shoved the bottle to my helper, swam to the gangway and climbed on board to investigate. As soon as I stepped on deck it hit me!"

With this last remark, Peter slapped the open

palm of his right hand against his forehead and paused. Spellbound, we were pinned to the edge of our seats, anxiously waiting for Peter to continue.

"What was it?" one of us asked impatiently.

"Well," Peter explained, "You see, after we passed the word for the passengers to go ashore so that we could deal with the head problem, we checked all the staterooms below to make sure no one was left behind and not using any of the toilets. This was done just before I went over the side with the diving bottle."

Peter took his Carib bottle from the table, held it up to the light and while squinting to study the contents, he spoke softly, "I had forgotten that we had a separate head on deck."

The expressions of anticipation on the faces of the audience now changed to devious grins. The occasional chuckle could be heard.

"Even though we had told everybody that the heads were out of order, this stupid woman was on it just when I let go with the diving bottle. When I opened the valve, all the stuff squirted out of the toilets and it practically lifted her off the seat."

We all howled with laughter.

"What happened to the lady, Peter?" someone asked.

"Oh well, initially we wrapped her in a blanket, but she reeked so badly that we threw her over the side for a good rinsing off."

Peter appeared to disapprove of the roars of laughter coming from his listeners. Annoyed, he added, "Well, it seemed the only decent thing to do, given the circumstances!"

Judy Kwaloff

There was an unusually large gathering in the Patio Bar of G.Y.S. The place was packed with skippers and crew of the various charter yachts anchored out in the lagoon and occupying the berths in the marina. We had just returned from a two week charter and my guests had been taxied to their hotel to spend a few days exploring Grenada before returning home. With the guests safely en route, I decided to find out what was brewing in the Patio Bar.

On my way to the Bar I noticed a large spill of paint on the dock, probably about a half a gallon. The paint covered an area of several square feet. With interest I noticed a legion of cockroaches situated along the edges of the paint spill. They appeared to be eating the stuff. For a while I watched and then continued on my way to the Patio Bar, cursing the idiot who had spilled the paint and neglected to clean it up. I intended to enquire about the culprit in the Patio Bar.

"Have you heard?" one of the skippers shouted at me, as I was welcomed into the group.

"Heard what? What's going on?" I shouted back. The place was noisy, the bar's reggae music coming from the stereo was cranked up high, and the loud voices of the many yachties, encouraged by a constant flow of spirits, added to the melee.

"Come over here!" the man yelled, as he waved me to a table where several skippers appeared to be loudly involved in agitated discussion.

(My memory is a bit vague about who exactly was there, so I may be placing the wrong people in the wrong location. Also, the exact exchange of words and who said what at which time may be incorrect, but the general gist of the conversation resembled the following narrative.)

The man who had called me to his table was Gilbert, owner and operator of the French charter yacht *Snark.* The others I recognized as Frick of *Mizar*, Ken of *Ticonderoga*, Bruno of the motor yacht *Mocambo*, Bert of *Dana*, Martin of *Bahari*, Jimmy of *Ariels,* and Debbie, skipperess of the yacht *Orphee.* This appeared to be the nucleus; others stood around and came and went as they shouted their comments to other groups who were also involved in what turned out to be the same hot topic.

"Sit down!" Gilbert commanded close to my ear, as he produced a chair which he pinched from another table whose customer had gone to the bar to refill his glass.

With bits and pieces gathered from the contingent seated at the table, frequently added to by those who came and went, I learned that the Government of Grenada had announced that a heavy tax would be imposed on the charter fees collected by the yachts. It was obvious that this announcement was received by the charter operators with much displeasure. As the others continued to loudly state their disapproval about the announcement, this frequently spiced with comments such as,"They can shove it where it sticks," I digested the news. It was bad news alright. The government had no right to do this. None of the yachts were Grenadian registry. None of the operators were local residents. None of them were employed in Grenada. The yachts travelled from island to island. Each island is a different country. The reason for the large concentration of charter yachts in Grenada was on account of the many things the island had to offer: good shelter and safe moorage, good repair facilities. Hurricanes are less likely to hit Grenada. In return, we spend a lot of money in Grenada. Most of our provisioning was done here. I steadily employed eight Grenadian crew and hired workers on a daily basis when in port. We paid moorage and haul out fees. Most charters ended in Grenada, and in most cases the guests stayed in a local hotel for at least a few days to explore the island, as was the case with the group we had just dropped off. All of the other boats operated in a similar manner. What concerned me most was that if Grenada got away with this latest scheme, what would the other islands do? They might want to jump on the band wagon and charge a tax too! As far as I was concerned the situation was intolerable. But what could we do? I prodded Ken who was now sitting closest to me.

"You got any suggestions?" My question was overheard by one of the others, who replied,"Naw, just don't pay it, no big deal!"

"That won't work," interjected Gilbert, "eventually that'll lead to all kinds of trouble."

"I agree," said Debbie,"They might seize the boat."

"Bull shit!" commented Bruno,"If they do that, they'll be in a pack of trouble. *Mocambo* is registered in Germany. It'll create an international incident!"

"Jah, sure," said Ken imitating a German accent,"Die Führer vill come und help!"

"Sieg Heil," shouted Bert, who had been following the conversation. "Let's revive the Gestapo and straighten out this mess!" He started parading around the patio bar in time with the reggae music and was promptly joined by several others. When the tune ended, the crowd settled down to replenish their drinks.

"We have to organize," I said during a moment of calm.

"Organize?" Ken repeated. "What are you talking about, join a union? Are you crazy?"

"No not exactly, but—" I wasn't quite sure what I meant, but an idea was forming in my head. "Maybe a club or something, a group. All I know is that individually we won't get anywhere, but maybe as a body— a group, we can talk to the Government and put some pressure on."

"I think you've got something there," said Bert, who had rejoined the table. "One person representing all the charter operators."

"Why not?" said Ken, "It's worth a try, nothing ventured, nothing gained!" He stood up and shouted at the top of his voice,

"Everybody, listen!"

As the crowed started to pay attention, Ken turned to the bartender and yelled, "Turn down that bloody music! We have something important to talk about!"

With the music suddenly stopped, silence fell amongst the crowd.

"Listen!" said Ken, with great flourish, "Jan here," he pointed at me, "the skipper of the *Ring Andersen*, is going to talk to the big chief of Grenada, the honourable Prime Minister Eric Gary. He is going to represent all of us! That means that whatever deal he makes, you have to stand behind him, OK?"

"Wait a minute," I said. "Why am I the one who has to talk to Gary? How about some democracy here and we talk this over?"

"Well, it was your idea right? OK then, you are the chosen one." Turning to the crowd he asked, "Does everyone agree?"

"Yes!" they all shouted, and then one added, "We don't wanna pay the tax!"

"Hurray!" the chorus responded.

Well, I guess that was that! I had opened my mouth and now I had better come up with the goodies.

As I walked back to *Ring Andersen* and came once again upon the spot where the paint had been spilled, I suddenly remembered my intention of finding out who was responsible for the spill.

Completely escaped my mind, I thought and then noticed to my surprise that the paint had almost completely disappeared. A few globs were still left, but they were quickly disappearing as the cockroaches were devouring the substance. *Amazing*! *Those little guys appear to be able to survive on anything. Could it be that these ancient creatures would turn out to be our saviours and solve the earth's pollution problem?*

The next morning I phoned Government office and asked for an audience with the Prime Minister. I was questioned about my purpose and when I said that I represented the charter yachts and wanted to discuss the newly announced tax law, I was put on hold. After a few minutes' delay I was informed that Mr. Gary was unavailable, but I could schedule an appointment with a Mr. St. John, aide to the Prime Minister. I responded that I would be pleased to meet with the gentleman at his convenience. Much to my surprise I was told that the official would see me at ten o'clock that morning.

Mr. St. John sat behind a large desk, and while perusing an important looking document, absent-mindedly waved me to an opposite chair. I sat down and waited. After a few minutes had gone by and without looking up from his reading material he said, "So, you want to talk about the new tax law." It was more a statement than a question.

I wasn't quite sure how to address such a personage, was it your excellency or your honour, your majesty perhaps? I figured, sir, would be reasonably safe, so I replied,

"Yes, sir!" He kept on reading. He did not call the troops to have me thrown out of the office, so I assumed the form of address was acceptable. So far so good! I added, since we had not yet been officially introduced,

"My name is Jan de Groot, I am the owner

and operator of the yacht *Ring Andersen*, and—"

"Yes, I know who you are," he interrupted, "and I know your yacht quite well, beautiful ship! The *Ring Andersen* has been in Grenada for many years and we're quite proud to have her in our harbour.

Hm, I thought, *a good beginning, maybe we'll get somewhere.* The gent had put his papers down and was now smiling at me from across the desk.

"Well, sir," I said, "I'm here as a representative of all the charter yachts. We have some deep concerns about the taxes you plan to levy against the yacht operators."

"Of course," he answered "Nobody likes to pay taxes. But, you people are here enjoying our island, an island which belongs to the Grenadian people. You should look at your stay in Grenada as a privilege. In return for this privilege we feel justified in charging you a tax so that you will contribute to our economy."

"I agree," I replied diplomatically, "Grenada is a beautiful country and we feel privileged with being here and receiving your splendid hospitality, but we do contribute to your economy in that we employ a large number of Grenadians who would otherwise be out of work, we patronize local merchants by buying provisions and materials for ship repair, and we bring tourists to the Island who spend money on hotels, sight seeing trips and so on. All this brings foreign currency into the island, most of it in the form of U.S. dollars."

I thought it would be wise not to mention the fact that all the yachts were of foreign registry and therefore technically foreign soil and to a large extend beyond the Government's jurisdiction. The man did not reply to my remarks but instead started reshuffling his papers. I took this as an opportunity to add some weight to the scale. I added, "You see sir, we do not conduct any business in Grenada. All our charters are from island to island, in other words, international, since each island is a different country. Our being here is no different from any cruising yacht which comes here to visit and while here, pays for the facilities offered."

"Yes," he replied, missing the point altogether," but the cruising yacht does not charter and does not earn money. They are here strictly for pleasure."

I tried to explain that made no difference, that while in Grenada we did not earn any money either, but to no avail. The man either did not see my point, or saw it alright, but had decided that he just didn't want to agree. I had run into this kind of situation with officials before and knew that arguing would not solve anything. We were at logger heads. His mind had been made up and a smallish minion like me was not about to change it. Furthermore, he was probably under pressure from his peers and may have been briefed not to give in. Thinking about the reception, which undoubtedly was anxiously awaiting me in the Patio Bar, I felt I had to throw in my last resource, secretly praying that what I was about to say would be backed up by those I represented. I scraped my throat and said, "Sir, it would be unfortunate if we can't solve this problem. I'm afraid that the group I represent is not willing to accept this taxation. On behalf of all the charter yacht operators, I'm sorry to have to inform you that unless the ruling is retracted, we'll have no alternative but to move the yachts to one of the other islands."

I waited for his response. When none came I stood up, thanked him politely for his time and walked to the door. I hoped that he would call me back, but he remained sitting there silently. I hesitated at the door, then opened it, and stepped out of his office. My taxi was waiting outside.

"Back to GYS," I said to Nelson, the cab driver.

"OK, Skip." answered Nelson, "How did it go, Skip?" Obviously the word had spread.

"Not so good," I replied, "But we shall see, it's not over yet!"

I looked at my watch, it was 10:25 A.M. It felt as if I had been with the official for hours, yet it had only been twenty five minutes. *Time goes quickly when you're having fun,* I thought. Some fun! The mob at GYS would probably lynch me when they heard the news.

It was only a short ride back to the Marina. The whole group was waiting for me at the entrance gate.

"Better sit down somewhere," I said, as I got out of the taxi. "I don't have very good news!"

"Why, what happened?" someone said.

"I'll tell you about it in a minute. Let's go to the Patio Bar." The bar was only a few strides away from the gate. Soon the whole group migrated

to the area which had become our head quarters. When everyone had gathered around me,
I gave them a report on the discussion I had
with the Prime Minister's representative. When
I told them that I had said that we would leave
the Island unless the tax law was changed, to
my surprise they applauded and cheered.

"Good for you!" some of them shouted, "Sock
it to them!"

With a sigh of relief, I said, "I'm glad you
agree, but now we have to put our money where
our mouth is. So I suppose we should give them
some time to respond and then, if nothing happens, we'll have to leave."

"No way," one of them said, "Let's show them
we mean business, let's leave right now!"

"Right now?" someone asked.

"Yes," several yelled in unison, "Let's go for
it."

After a short discussion it was decided that
unless we received an official retraction of the
tax law by 1300 hrs, we would take our boats
and head out of the harbour.

At 1 o'clock in the afternoon, the little customs office in the Marina was crowded with
skippers filing the necessary clearance papers.
I felt certain that our activities were being re-
layed to the dignitaries at Government house.
At about 2 o'clock, I believe some forty odd,
although some claim the number was closer to
eighty, big yachts motored out of the harbour
and then headed north along the West Coast of
Grenada. By the time we reached the northern
end of Grenada, an announcement came
through on the public broadcasting system that

the tax law had been reviewed and deemed in-appropriate, would the charter yachts therefore please return to Grenada!

The good news was passed along to those who had not been listening to the Grenada radio sta-tion. The flotilla doubled back on their course and all boats were soon re-secured to their favourite moorings. That night the Red Crab, the yachties favourite night time pub, was packed with the cel-ebrating troops from the charter yachts.

Not too long after this event and probably due to its favourable outcome, the Caribbean Charter Yacht Association was formed. The ideal person to administer this Association was Judy Kwaloff.

Judy Kwaloff first operated from St. Vincent and later on from Bequia, a small Island just south of St. Vincent. She had been a charter agent, originally operating from the U.S.A., but had relocated her business, Windward Island Tours, to the Caribbean because she too preferred the life style and climate of the islands. Judy was of Jewish descent and having grown up in the Big Apple, she spoke with a strong New York ac-cent. She was petite, dark haired, and had a cheerful couldn't-care-less attitude. Judy was very outspoken, business like, and had no pa-tience for fools. If someone got on the wrong side of her, she would set that person straight in short order, no ifs or buts! But underneath her bra-vado and intimidating manner, it was known to all of us who knew her well, that above all, she had a heart of gold! The best way to describe Judy is probably demonstrated in the name she had given to her sailing boat. She had named it

Bucket. When I asked her what on earth inspired her to come up with that name, she answered, "Because that is the closest I could come to, Fuck it!"

Judy's business as charter agent was not flourishing. Having left the U.S. where most of her clients resided, she was out of touch and unable to provide proper service. The majority of her clientele went elsewhere; only a faithful few remained. Communication between the Islands and the rest of the world was poor, the local telephone system being of outdated design. This also hindered the charter yachts operating in the area, since it was difficult for the charter skippers, who were constantly on the move, to coordinate the dates of the charters booked for them by the agents who were actively booking. Through the Caribbean Charter Yacht Association it was now possible to solve this problem. It was decided to establish a shore based office which would act as representative for all the boats. All charters booked for the boats would be channelled through this office. This would make it easier for the agents and also for the charter operators. Judy, who had been instrumental in organizing this facility, was the perfect person to manage this operation. As a result, Judy became the manager of the Association. She ruled it with an iron fist.

The C.C.Y.A., or to be exact, Judy's office, soon became the centre of activity. This is where boats gathered to await instructions for new charters. This is where the contracts were received and signed, and more importantly, where the charter fees were paid to the charter operators. Judy's idea of running this office went well beyond the call of duty. Judy recruited many a new arrival in the business. When anyone had a problem, Judy was always there to listen or give advice and lend a helping hand. Crew looking for work soon found that Judy could find them a job and in the mean time, she would serve them a meal and give them a bed. If a charter yacht skipper needed a crew, she always knew just the right person for the job. She knew everybody and everybody knew her. We loved her and we miss her. Judy died of cancer in 1986.

Bride and Groom

Here comes the bride

Daughter Karen at the wheel

Family Matters

Sometimes one can wake up in the morning and find that a chance meeting has changed the entire course of one's life. A few developments of note in my personal life should be mentioned to clarify why certain people were in a certain place at a certain time. So, let me explain.

When I first went to Grenada to take the *Ring Andersen* on her trip to Tobago, David Collyer was part of the permanent crew and functioned as my right hand. David helped entertain the guests, took care of the administration and payroll, and basically jumped in wherever needed. In the mean time, my wife Elise and my two daughters, Michele and Karen, were still in Vancouver awaiting the outcome of my exploits in the sunny Caribbean. Soon, I signalled the green light. Suitable tenants were found for the house in Vancouver and Elise and the girls joined me on the *Ring Andersen.* For awhile they joined us on the charters, but Karen, at age eight, and Michele, being her senior by only two years, required education. It was therefore decided that we needed a shore base so that the girls could attend a local school. David felt it was time for him to move on and get down to the business of pursuing a serious

career. At least that was his excuse. I suspect
the real reason was a young lady with whom
he had been corresponding at an alarming rate.
After all, absence makes the heart grow fonder.
Much to my regret we saw David off at the
airport for his flight back to Vancouver. We
rented a house in Grenada and the girls went
to a local school. As much as possible, Elise
accompanied me on charters, taking on David's
duties. Then, political tension began to rise in
the Island due to the forthcoming independence from Great Britain. As a result, most of
the expatriates living in Grenada moved to
St.Vincent. We followed and rented accommodation in St. Vincent. When the unrest settled
down we moved back to Grenada. After a while,
Elise became disenchanted with our unstable
lifestyle and, I think, particularly with her fickle
husband who was having a good time cruising,
she decided to return to the civilized world and
enrolled the girls in their normal school curriculum. In order to help support our two home
base lifestyles, Elise found a job which settled
her back in a familiar routine. During stretches
when the *Ring Andersen* was not busy with
charters, I would fly to Vancouver and join the
family for short periods. Needless to say, this
was not an ideal situation. Elise did not fancy
returning to the Caribbean, unless the girls
went to a boarding school to receive a proper
education. I did not like the boarding school
idea and could not abandon the *Ring Andersen*
at a moment's notice. In fact, we had come to a
crossroads of which the future route was
impossible to choose. To make matters more

complicated, Elise had become very friendly with her boss, a charming and hard working fellow whose feet were firmly embedded in the establishment. The whole situation came to an abrupt end when during one of my visits to Vancouver, Elise took a glance at the crew list which I had brought with me to obtain visas from the American Consulate for *Ring's* forthcoming trip to U.S. territory. On the list was a name, Naomi, obviously a female! In fact, Naomi was a girl I had signed on as a deck hand since she needed a ride to the Virgin Islands where she would disembark. There were no romantic implications involved. However, the incident added fuel to the fire and, poof, our castle of marriage came crumbling down.

During the absence of David and later Elise, I ran the charters on *Ring* strictly with my Grenadian crew. The presence of Elise during previous charters made me aware that a charter is smoother and more successful with a female crew member on board. The female touch is important on a charter yacht, especially for the lady guests who have certain secret requirements which are more easily divulged to a female crew member. Also for the men, the combination of host and hostess adds to that little extra that creates the intimate atmosphere, which is desirable for the perfect charter.

We were booked to do a charter in tandem with the *Dana*, which was operated by my friend Bert and his wife Lenny. We were to do a series of short, daily trips along the south coast of

Grenada. This was a company group, similar to the Insurance Company which we had entertained in Tobago. The group was staying in the Holiday Inn and, daily, about eighty people would be delivered to us by bus: forty for *Dana* and forty for us. For this little escapade I needed help. By chance it so happened that a young lady, whom I had met once before, had left the boat she had been working on. She was available for two weeks after which she would be hitching a ride on a racing yacht destined for the Mediterranean. She had a boyfriend awaiting her in the Mediterranean. I signed her on for the two weeks and agreed to sail her to Antigua where our next charter was to begin and where the boat she would be joining was undergoing some work to ready her for the long voyage. Julian, better known to her friends as Jules, is British and was trained in hotel management. She originally came to the Caribbean when she was hired as assistant manager of a resort on the Island of Bequia. Due to certain circumstances during her employ, Julian decided that she didn't wish to remain with the resort and signed on as a crew member on a charter yacht. She roamed the Caribbean for some time and then ended up in Gibraltar and later Cyprus where she managed a restaurant. Later, she returned to the Caribbean. It was during her second term in the islands that we met and she agreed to help out during the tandem charter.

As I was soon to find out, she was an excellent hostess and a superb cook. After we finished the day trips with *Dana*, we departed for Antigua to pick up the charter party awaiting us there. On the way up, Jules was notified by radio that her ride to the Mediterranean had been delayed due to some complications with the fitting out of the racing yacht. As a result, and to my delight, Jules remained on board and welcomed our guests in Antigua. My newly found crew member took to *Ring* and guests as the true professional she was. This, combined with her extremely attractive appearance, made me plot a scheme that would keep her on *Ring* on a permanent basis. It took some time, but, you guessed it, the result was a wedding ceremony performed on board while we cruised off the coast of Grenada.

When the wedding plans were announced, many of the local yachties participated with the offering of help and ideas to make it a memorable occasion. When, with all the enthusiastic input of the yachting fraternity, things took on the tendency of getting a little out of hand, Jack McKitrick jovially told me not to worry. He would take care of all the arrangements. Jack was at that time the skipper of the motor yacht *Kalizma*, which was originally owned by the actress, Elizabeth Taylor. Relieved, I entrusted Jack with the organization of the actual ceremony. He decided on what turned out to be his version of a fully uniformed naval-type-wedding. The fact that I no longer possessed a uniform was no problem, Jack would arrange for one. Jules, in the mean time, located and purchased a beautiful wedding dress in the boutique, on the island of Mustique. Jules' parents confirmed that they would fly over from England. Michele, my eldest daughter, who was living with us and taking a correspondence course, was to be bride's maid and Haze Richardson from the Petit St.Vincent resort agreed to be Best Man. The next task was to find a minister who would perform the actual ceremony, not in church, but on the boat while under sail. We soon found our man, no problem, but one small favour, he had eleven children, could they come too? Their ages ranged from diaper stage to sixteen years. Jules and I looked at each other. This could present a big problem. All those little tykes running around on a crowded ship, anything could happen. We managed to convince the minister that this was not a good idea. He could bring the children on board some other time for a visit while the boat was safely tied to the dock. Much to our relief, he agreed. To aid our crew with the additional catering we hired extra hands for the big day. One of the extras was Sam, the chef of another charter yacht. Sam, a native of Grenada, was a fellow with a happy disposition and very forgiving about the idiosyncrasies of the Caucasian way of living. Jules had stashed away on board a few bottles of a very expensive champagne. These she had been saving for a special occasion. Well, if there ever was a special occasion, nothing could be more special than our wedding day. Jules decided that Sam would be the ideal person to present the treasure at the right moment. She explained to Sam that he was to open the bottles at the precise moment when the minister had pronounced us husband and wife. She was concerned, though, about the corks. Jules was afraid that the corks might pop off and hit somebody. She therefore instructed Sam to open the bottles on the outside of the railings so that the corks would end up in the ocean rather than in someone's eye. Agreeably, Sam said that he would do as the mistress asked. When later the bottles were opened right on cue, we observed Sam firing off the corks and then pouring the precious contents into the ocean! When the deed was done, he turned to us with a proud smile. Oops, a slight misunderstanding! Sam thought this was one of those crazy things that us white folks do, some ritual, pouring the champagne into the sea. All things considered it was probably a good omen, because the whole affair went smoothly. I must say that I had a moment's hesitation when we, the happy couple, were to walk through an arch of Jack McKitrick's uniformed naval officers who stood lined up with swords stretched, but none of the swords came down and we managed to parade through unscathed. I did notice, though, that Jack and the others were in shirt sleeves, whereas Jack had insisted that I wear the heavy jacket that came with the uniform. A mischievous smile appeared on Jack's face every time he looked at the perspiration streaming down my cheeks caused by the combination of heavy attire and tropical heat.

When we returned from our cruise in the early hours of the evening, the band came on board and the party began. I lost count of the numbers of well wishers which ranged from taxi drivers and dock boys to government dignitaries. The party lasted until the wee hours of the morning. The whole day had been an enormous success. Both my new bride and I where delighted. This truly had been the best wedding anyone could have hoped for.

My divorce from Elise had been resolved amicably. To this day we remain good friends. This benefitted everyone involved, especially the girls. With mutual agreement they were free to choose where they wanted to reside. Michele elected to come to the Caribbean and stay with us. Karen, the youngest, stayed in school in Canada but would join us every summer holiday. I was delighted to have at least one of the girls on board on a permanent basis. But it did have some complications. As she grew up, her pretty, tall blond features did not go unnoticed.

She was soon given undivided attention by Jonathan, one of the crew members of *Kalizma*, which was now skippered by Peter Davis, not to be confused with the Peter Davies whom I referred to in one of the earlier chapters. Jonathan, a nice lad from South Africa who was seeing the world by crewing on charter yachts, was in my somewhat biased opinion too worldly for my precious daughter. I watched the couple with suspicion and checked every move they made. My over zealous father instinct was the cause of a rather embarrassing development. I had been visiting on one of the other boats tied up in the marina. It was rather late and I climbed quietly back on board, being careful to not awaken anyone. Before entering our cabin, where Jules was soundly asleep, I peeked into Michele's cabin. To my horror I noticed that her bunk was empty. Alarmed, I awakened Jules.

"Where is Michele?" I exclaimed.

"What are you talking about?" Jules mumbled, still half asleep.

"Michele, where is she?"

"Isn't she in her cabin?" Jules, now wide awake and alert, asked with alarm in her voice. One look at the expression of panic on my face prompted her to immediate action. She jumped out of her bunk and hastily threw on some clothes. "My God, where could she be?" Jules shouted as she ran to Michele's cabin to make sure that I had not lost my senses.

"I know where she is," I grunted, "she must be with that Jonathan. I'll kill that no good son of a—!" I raced up the stairs, then onto the deck, jumped over the bulwarks and ran to the dock where the *Kalizma* was tied up. A light was on in the salon. Normally one would knock on the hull and wait to be invited on board. No time for formalities now. I ran up the gangway, then up to the deck where the salon was situated and opened the door. Once inside, Peter Davis, who had been seated in a comfortable chair, looked up from the book he had been reading with a startled expression. Before he could ask what the heck I was doing bursting in like that, I demanded,"Where is Jonathan?"

"Why, what's going on?" Peter obviously realized that I was under some stress. Trying to calm me down he offered me a chair.

"Never mind that," I said, declining the gesture, "Michele is missing and I bet she is with that crewman of yours, Jonathan. He must have lured her into his cabin and no good will come of that."

"Simmer down, Jan," Peter said, trying to calm me down. "Jonathan is sound asleep in his cabin and I'm certain Michele isn't with him."

"How do you know that? Have you checked?"

"No, but Jonathan went to his bunk at least two hours ago. He said good night to me when he turned in and Michele was not with him."

"Well—eh—where is his cabin, I want to see if that is so!"

"No, I will go and check on him if you insist. Why don't you sit down in that chair and calm down."

Peter left and I started pacing the salon. Soon Peter returned.

"Well?" I questioned.

"No, Jan, Michele is not here. It's as I said, Jonathan was sound asleep, alone," he added. "But," he continued, "I've woken him up because we'd better start a search party. We'll be over shortly."

His last remark brought a new wave of panic. Holy smokes! If Michele was not with Jonathan, then where the heck was she? I returned to the *Ring Andersen*. By now the various yachties were being awakened by the commotion and had started to gather on *Ring's* decks. We discussed the various possibilities of Michele's disappearance and started to form a search plan when suddenly we heard a voice.

"Dad!"

I could not determine where the sound came from. We all fell quiet and listened.

"Michele," I called, "where are you?"

"Here dad. Why is there so much noise? Is something wrong?"

"For God's sake, Michele, where are you?" I repeated. And then I saw her. She appeared to be hovering in the darkness like a white ghost, well above our heads, but about thirty feet forward of where we were gathered. I realized she was standing on the deck house wrapped in a white bed sheet.

"Where have you been and what are you doing up there?" I demanded.

"It was too hot in my cabin so I decided to sleep up here. Out here it is much cooler," she spoke as she carefully came down the ladder holding the bed sheet with one hand for cover. I rushed over to her and with great relief held her tightly wrapped in my arms.

The crisis now having come to a happy ending, the crowd disbursed to their various yachts to resume their interrupted night's rest.

Occasionally, I still get teased about the erratic behaviour I displayed during this incident.

The Flag

In 1974, Grenada separated from British rule and became an independent state within the Commonwealth. The whole procedure had been the subject of much adverse publicity. As the island went through some disorder, because of disagreement over the issue amongst local political parties, foreign news media had their heyday. Hordes of journalists invaded the island looking for sensational articles to send back to their employers. Those who couldn't find suitable stories to write made them up with little concern for the truth. The final result was the presentation of a picture to the outside world which incorrectly gave the impression that the new nation's problems were racial, rather than a political disagreement between the local factions. In actual fact, the problems had no effect on the foreigners who were residing on the island, nor were the tourists vacationing in Grenada, threatened or in danger at any time.

One journalist was so frustrated by the fact that the situation was so mellow in relation to his expectations that he decided to stir up some trouble on his own. He arrived after independence day and after the few local demonstrations staged by the opposing party had already taken place. The odd skirmishes resulting from these demonstrations would barely have made the local news had they occurred in a city such as Chicago or New York.

The reporter wouldn't settle for this. After all, he had readers back home who were eager for excitement, sensation and blood! Furthermore, only good stories sell. That means the gorier the better. He managed to sneak into a closed meeting of the ruling party held at the banquet room of the Holiday Inn.

The gathering was chaired by the Prime Minister, Sir Eric Gary. Several times the clandestine guest interrupted the proceedings by loudly making derogatory remarks and demanding answers to offensive questions. Although he had no business being present at the function in the first place, the officials allowed him to stay, but did point out that this was not a press conference nor a public meeting, so would he kindly not interfere with the agenda and keep quiet.

This, however, was not what the eager beaver had come for. He kept interrupting and eventually became downright abusive. The result was that a policeman had to be called to remove him from the proceedings.

The next morning, the reporter was overheard in the hotel's dining room insulting the country's government and its inhabitants in a loud voice. The hotel manager, who had witnessed the man's belligerent behaviour of the previous day, was so disgusted with his nuisance guest that he told him to pack his suitcase and leave the hotel.

Some days later, we read the 'journalist's' report which he had been able to peddle to the *New York Times*. He talked in the article of having attended a press conference and being arrested and tortured by the Mongoose Gang because of having asked questions pertinent to the nation's politics. He also managed to create the impression that the place was in terrible turmoil and that bombs were exploding at the local airport. He had escaped by the skin of his teeth!

Unfortunately, the article was repeated by many other newspapers. The result was that the reading public took the man's lies for the gospel truth and avoided the island like the plague. For several years the tiny nation suffered from a lack of much needed tourist income.

While the angry hotel manager bid his farewells to the irresponsible reporter, the yacht *Ring Andersen* approached the entrance to the harbour of St.George's, Grenada's capital city.

"See the flag, Skip?" Thomas asked.

"What flag?" I mumbled. I was concentrating on the antics of a couple of local fishing boats who threatened to obstruct my view of the range marker which indicated the entrance to the tricky channel we had to manoeuvre through. Perfect alignment to enter the narrow channel was of vital importance. The crew of the fishing boats noticed our approach and moved out of the way. Relieved, I turned to Thomas, alias Steam Box.

"What flag?" I asked again.

"Look, over there, on the *Fort*." Thomas answered, pointing at *Fort George*, which is perched on the top of a bluff at the harbour entrance.

"Ah yes, I see. Looks quite impressive. It must be the new flag of Grenada."

"I think so, Skip," Thomas remarked, as he turned away to help the other crew with the chores of preparing the yacht for coming alongside the dock at the marina.

We were arriving with six American charter guests who had been on board for the past seven days. They would be with us for another three days in Grenada. These extra days would be spent touring the island before going back to the States.

As we slowly proceeded through the channel, I kept thinking of the new flag. I must confess, I have a weakness for flags. I find them attractive and fascinating. I've gathered a small collection of these cheerful objects. Just before coming alongside the dock, I threw another hasty glance at the fort and looked at the now distant colours flying in the breeze. When we were securely tied up, I picked up the binoculars and once again studied the new flag. *There probably are not too many of those around as yet,* I thought. *I wonder how I can get one.*

A few moments later, Mr. John, the customs and immigration officer stepped on board to perform the formalities necessary to give legal entrance into the country. After he had put the final stamps and signatures on our crew and passenger manifest, he stood up, shook my hand and said,"Welcome back to Grenada, captain. Yours is the first ship to enter the port since our country has become independent."

"Really, Mr John, are you certain about that?"

"Yes, I'm quite certain. See, here is my log book. This is the first entry since the celebrations."

Mr. John allowed me a quick inspection of the carefully written pages of his treasured token of authority. With respect I examined his entries. When he decided I had seen enough, he closed the book with a snap, wished my guests a pleasant stay and took his leave.

Once more, I took the binoculars out of their case and studied the flag flying on the Fort.

Maybe, we've got ourselves a flag, I thought. I put the glasses back in their place and walked to the dock office. I looked through the telephone book and dialled the number.

"Office of the Prime Minister," the voice answered.

"I would like a meeting with the Prime Minister, " I said.

"One moment, please." A minute went by and another voice said,

"Can I help you?"

"I would like a meeting with the Prime Minister," I repeated.

"What is your name and why do you want to see him? This is the Prime Minister's aide."

"My name is Jan de Groot of the yacht *Ring Andersen.* I need to see the Prime Minister regarding an urgent matter which l cannot discuss over the telephone."

There was a momentary silence on the other side of the line and then the official asked,"How urgent is it?"

"Very urgent. It is necessary that I see him today!"

Again, the telephone went silent. I waited patiently until the man came back with, "Where are you phoning from?"

"From the office of Grenada Yacht Services."

"Oh, I see. What is the number there?"

"Two, four, three."

"I will call you back."

The phone clicked and went silent. I put down the receiver and walked back to the boat. About half an hour later, I was called to the phone.

"Is this Captain de Groot of the *Ring Andersen*?"

"That's right," I replied.

"The Prime minister will see you at three o'clock this afternoon."

"Great," I answered, "I'll be there."

Back on board, I explained my plan to my friend, Tom de Roos. Tom was taking a vacation from a very busy medical practice in Vancouver and had been crewing on *Ring* for several months. To make his presence official, he was signed onto the crew manifest as ship's doctor. Tom listened to my plan of attack and broke out in laughter when I finished.

"You're out of your mind, Jan?" he chuckled. "He'll never go for it and you will end up on the hill!" With this remark he pointed towards the local jail which is situated on the mountain overlooking the harbour. I could still hear his laugh when I had gone below to spruce up for the pending encounter.

A taxi took me to Government House. A guard at the gate asked my name and allowed me to proceed. I met the illustrious Sir Eric Gary just as he stepped onto the veranda fronting the main entrance of the colonial type mansion. He was dressed in his trademark, an immaculately pressed white suit. He jovially shook my hand and said, "So, you are the owner of the yacht *Ring Andersen?*"

"Yes, sir," I answered and thought, *Hm, somebody has done his home work.*

"Such a nice yacht! The *Ring Andersen* has been coming to our country for quite some time. We look upon the yacht as being Grenadian. The harbour would not be the same without her. I have been onboard her many times, you know. But that was before you owned her."

The chit chat went on as we leisurely walked through the well groomed gardens of the estate. Mr. Gary did the talking and I tuned in with the appropriate,"Yes" and "No," here and there. Abruptly, he broke off the conversation and looked at his watch.

"Well, it is time for me to go. I have an appointment. What is this urgent matter you want to see me about?"

This time I did the talking while he listened. I explained that since the island had received a lot of bad publicity lately, which no doubt would hurt the tourist business, there was now an excellent opportunity for the Prime Minister to prove to the world that tourists were very welcome in Grenada. All he had to do was to welcome *Ring Andersen* as the first ship to arrive in Grenada since independence day. My guests would still be onboard for a few more days, so he could announce Grenada's hospitality to them as well. I suggested the occasion be celebrated with a flag raising ceremony whereby the Prime Minister would present the new flag of the nation to me as a symbol of the event. Since there still were many people of the news media on the island, no doubt the ceremony would be televised and reported to many corners of the world.

Mr. Gary had listened to my proposal without interruption.

"Look," he said, "I'm already late for an appointment. Let's meet for lunch tomorrow at the Rock Gardens. You know where that is, don't you?"

I knew the place well enough. The Rock Gardens is a restaurant owned by Mr. Gary. I agreed to meet him the next day at one o'clock. We said goodbye and I returned to the yacht basin.

The next day I met the Prime Minister in his restaurant. We moved to a table in the back of the establishment and made a selection from the menu.

Again, he started chit chatting, with me sticking to the oh's and ah's. When the waitress came with the order and bent over to put the plates on the table, I noticed Sir Eric take the opportunity to pinch her bum. Apparently, the girl was used to it, because she made no fuss. When a while later she returned to tend to our table, he winked at me while his hand disappeared under her skirt. The girl giggled and moved away to another table.

Eventually, I managed to turn the subject of our discussion to the presentation of the flag. To my relief, he informed me that he had given the idea some thought and had decided to be on board the next morning at ten o'clock for the ceremony. The entire cabinet would be present and the press had been advised.

The luncheon went on for another two hours and when I started to look at my watch, Sir Eric said, "Good heavens, look at the time." He stood up, said "Good bye," and left. As if by magic, the restaurant's bill appeared in front of me. I peeled the money from my wallet and put it on the table, including a tip for the waitress with the sore bum.

Happy with my victory, I hurried back to the yacht to tell the good news. We advised the guests of the forthcoming events, and that evening Tom and I drank a toast to the new flag which would soon be added to the collection.

The ceremony was a success. Not only did we acquire the desired flag, but Sir Eric Gary also presented me with a large print of the new Coat of Arms. Later, I learned that only eight such prints were made of this emblem, which was produced and designed by the British Heraldic Society. The prints were made at great expense with the understanding that thousands more would be ordered. Since the island's treasury did not have the funds to place the order, no others were printed. Apparently, of the eight copies printed, one was given to the Governor General, one to me and the other six were, I was told, maliciously destroyed. That makes my copy a very rare collector's item indeed.

I had the privilege of enjoying several more meals with the Prime Minister. The lunches were held in The Rock Gardens, the dinners served in The Palace, another restaurant owned by Sir

Sir Eric presents the flag

Eric. The meals were accompanied by a vast amount of pinched rear ends, and I had become accustomed to picking up the tab.

It is amazing how a tiny misinterpretation can grow into a giant misunderstanding. Some months later I made a short visit to Vancouver where I met a friend, who by the grape vine had heard of my association with Grenada's political leader. The name of Sir Eric Gary's other restaurant, The Palace, had thrown an interesting twist to the imagination of some of my Vancouver acquaintances. It was rumoured that I had become such good friends with Grenada's head of state that I was now living in the Palace! This, of course, was quite hilarious, although at one time, I came fairly close to the nearest thing.

During one of the lunches, Sir Eric offered me the post of Minister of Tourism. I thanked him for the honour but made some polite excuses for reasons of self preservation. The regime was, in my opinion, a bit unstable. I felt it was better not to get involved in local politics, nor did I want my head chopped off in the event the ruling party became target practice for the opposition. Fortunately, we were soon to embark on a series of charters which would take us away from the Island for several months. This provided me with a good opportunity to cool the relationship with Sir Eric. Considering Maurice Bishop's coup d'etat a few years later, I probably made the right decision.

The Skipper

It is important that the skipper keeps his cool at all times. He must appear to be in control of the situation always, even when he isn't. On a charter yacht this rule is even more important. Nothing is more alarming to the passengers than a skipper who panics when something goes wrong. Some yachtsmen have the annoying habit of yelling and shouting in certain situations, such as coming along side a dock. It usually is an indication of incompetence of the skipper, not the crew. This phenomenon can be witnessed often when watching boats coming into a marina. The nervous skipper who sails with his wife can usually be recognised even when he is still several yards away from the docking space.

"Mary, don't forget the fenders. Mary, the fenders! Mary, tie them to the railing! To the railing! Mary, no, no, not there! Further back, further back, I said! Yes, there! Now, when we get to the dock, you jump and tie the bow line to the dock cleat. You got that? Okay, now, Mary! Now! Jump! Jesus Christ, Mary! You didn't tie the mooring line to the boat!"

A variation to this is the boat with two skippers.

"Mary, when we come along side, I want the bowline onshore first."

"Why?"

"Because that is the best way to do it."

"I don't think so. I think it makes much more sense to get the stern line tied on first."

"How can I manoeuvre the boat if the stern is tied to the dock, Mary?"

"That's your problem, you are at the helm. It is much easier for me to jump from the stern and the bowline is not long enough for me to jump with it from here."

"Oh, for Pete's sake, Mary, why don't you do as I ask for once?"

"Well, you jump off the bow then. You want to be the Captain, you tie up this damn boat. I have to go below anyway, the kettle is boiling!"

I am not sure which of the two situations is worse, probably the second one. If at all possible, I like to have my boat a safe distance away from either docking procedures.

Obviously, this type of behaviour does not in- still much confidence in the charter guests who are waiting on shore to embark for a vacation on the high seas.

The seasoned skipper has no cause for yelling and shouting at his crew. His operation is that of a well oiled machine—everything goes with preci- sion and planning. He thinks and plans ahead. Should anything go wrong, he keeps his cool and quickly decides a different course of action. The cool cat is the skipper who will run his boat aground in front of an audience and make it appear as if he did it on purpose. I heard a story of a guy whose craft went aground during an outgoing tide. He lit up his pipe and while puffing away, told his crew that he usually did some work on the boat in this area. He launched the dinghy, picked up a can of paint and a brush and started painting the yacht's bottom as it dried above the falling tide.

On *Ring Andersen* we used a system of hand signals and whistles. One long whistle meant we were about to tack. One short whistle indicated 'helm down', two short whistles 'let go running back stays and sheets,' and three whistles, 'secure windward running backstay and trim sheets for the new course'. Hand signals were given for further sail trimming and picking up the anchor. It worked perfectly, with never a spoken word.

Keeping up the pretence of being the 'forever cool and collected skipper' for the sake of the charter guests can sometimes be a trying experience.

We pulled up anchor at a calm anchorage on the south west side of St.Kits. We sailed up the leeward side of the island, rounded the northern end and set course for the French Island, St.Barts. A brisk wind was blowing at about 30 knots, but *Ring* carried her sail well, so we kept everything up. The wind direction was such that we could make the thirty odd mile crossing on one tack. The yacht was heeled over at a comfortable angle and moved as if she was being chased by the devil. The sky was clear and we all enjoyed the exhilarating sail. Most of us were a little disappointed when the harbour of St.Barts hove into sight. When we came close to the land, I signalled the crew to take the sails down and luffed up into the wind. On the signal, Thomas descended into the engine room and started the iron genny. When he came back on deck he looked like King Neptune. He was soaking wet and dripping with dirty oily water. He looked at me with eyes as large as saucers. I wondered if he had just met the Lochness monster. I looked at the guests who were all on deck within earshot, watching the sites on the shoreline. I took a deep breath and said calmly,

"Come over here, Thomas."

Mesmerised, he stepped beside me at the wheel. With as normal a face as I could muster, I whispered in his ear,

"What the hell is going on down there?"

"There's water coming from everywhere, Skip."

"What do you mean, from everywhere?"

"Just like I said Skip, from everywhere. It just comes from all over the place!"

My mind raced a mile a minute. *Must have sprung a plank*, I thought. The charter guests were now looking at the dripping Thomas instead of the sites on shore. I bent down to disengage the clutch to stop the propeller from turning and took the opportunity to whisper once more to our soaked engineer,

"Go get Raphael," and added, "QUICKLY!"

Thomas disappeared and came back with our bosun. I turned to Thomas and told him to start the bilge pumps. He left to carry out the order. Raphael looked at me questioningly. I stuffed him in front of the wheel and said,

"You know this harbour, don't you?" Without

waiting for his reply I continued, "At the far end, on the north side, is a very shallow patch with a sandy bottom. You take the wheel and keep the boat in this position. I'm going down into the engine room. When I give the word, you run the ship straight onto that shallow spot, understand?"

"Yes Skip, I understand. Are we sinking, Skip?"

"Not if I can help it," I answered softly.

The charter guests had now become aware that something was amiss.

"Is anything wrong?" one of them asked.

"Just a small problem in the engine room," I answered with a straight face. "Broken pipe or something. Nothing to worry about. I am going to fix it now!"

I went down the ladder to investigate.

The situation was exactly as Thomas had described. Water appeared to be spraying in from all directions. Within seconds I was soaked from tip to toe. At first reaction, I was tempted to tell Raphael to head for the sand bank and beach the ship. But then I realised that the water could not possibly come from all directions at the same time. We obviously had a leak, but I should be able to isolate the area. I went further into the engine room and discovered what caused the water to be thrown around like a blizzard in the prairies. There was water in the bilge and it was being picked up and flung out by the large flywheel of the engine. I opened the floor boards to see where the water came from, but could not locate any area that looked suspicious. I could hear the pumps running and suddenly I noticed the water level going down. The fly wheel was now out of the water and no longer spraying it around. A few seconds later the pumps gurgled as they picked up air and the bilge was empty. For all the time it took for the pumps to work, there could not have been more than thirty buckets of water in the bilge. Quite acceptable for a hull the size of *Ring*. Then what had caused the deluge of water in the engine room?

As it turned out, there was a blockage in the drainage system which connects the engine room bilge with the well, a deeper spot where the water could be easier pumped out. When the yacht had been on the same tack and thus been heeled over at the same angle for a long time, water had gathered at the turn of the bilge in the engine room. When we suddenly luffed up to furl the sails, consequently allowing the yacht to level off to an even keel, the water ran to the small compartment underneath the flywheel. The partially clogged lumber holes had prevented the water from escaping to the well.

Not all charters turn out as a happy event for the charter guest. Fortunately, bad experiences are rare. If they do occur, it is usually due to an incapable skipper, never because of an inexperienced crew. If a boat has a good crew, there is a good skipper in charge. If the crew is sloppy, disorganized and untrained, it is the skipper's fault. The system is self-correcting. A good crew would not sail with a bad skipper. A good skipper would not tolerate a bad crew. He would train them or fire them. A typical example of 'bad skipper syndrome', is the case of the yacht, *National*.

National was a Baltic trader which had been converted to a pleasure vessel. She was a large and heavily constructed, seaworthy ship. Unfortunately, the vessel was owned by a jerk, who through poor seamanship showed that he had no regard for the safety of his ship or her passengers. *National* was based in St. Lucia were she was used to take large numbers of people out for day excursions. During one of the daytrips, some passengers who had enjoyed the daily outing were conned into chartering the vessel by her unscrupulous owner-skipper. The man might have been capable of running the boat on short day trips along St.Lucia's coastline, but he had no idea how to run a charter yacht in the reef infested waters of the southern island chain.

National had arrived in Admiralty Bay in the island of Bequia with ten charter guests on board. On Wednesday, at three o'clock in the afternoon, Captain Jerk was on shore talking with Mr. Simmons, the local sail maker. The fellow indicated to the island's old timer that he was going to Petit St.Vincent to attend the *jump up* that evening. A *jump up* is a West Indian name for a dance or party. The Wednesday evening jump ups at P.S.V. were a popular attraction for the charter yachts, as it provided West Indian type entertainment for both guests and crew alike. The tiny island is situated in an area which is difficult to navigate and almost next to the treacherous Tobago

Cays. Mr. Simmons, who realised that *National's* skipper was unfamiliar with the local waters, told the man that he could not go to the jump up, because it was too late in the day. It takes at least four hours to cover the distance from Bequia to Petit St. Vincent. As it is dark at six o'clock and even experienced sailors would sail that route at that time of day only in case of an extreme emergency, it was impossible for *National* to make the voyage at that late hour. Mr. Simmons explained all this to the novice, but he departed for his destination nevertheless, after signing on one additional crew member. He managed to get a girl by the name of Marie to join the crew as cook. Marie worked in the Frangipani, a local hotel and restaurant. She had not worked on boats before, but thought this might be a nice break from the daily routine. The hiring of Marie was the only sensible thing the ignorant skipper did.

National weighed anchor at approximately half past three and sailed out of Admiralty Bay. A while later, the yacht *Margay* also left the bay in the same general direction. The 60 foot catamaran *Margay* was a charter yacht operated by Dave Stone. Dave was a seasoned charter skipper who had been in the islands for several years. Dave also would have liked to go to P.S.V. but realising there was not enough light left in the day, he planned to overnight in Salt Whistle Bay, which is one of the anchorages in Mayero, an island en route to P.S.V. When Dave cleared the most western point of Admiralty Bay and rounded West Cay to proceed in a southerly direction, he could see *National* a few miles ahead of him. It was a usual blustery Caribbean day with a good bite to the wind and a bit rougher than normal seaway. The largest island encountered en route to P.S.V. is Cannouan. One normally passes this island to leeward to avoid the rough water and reef infested shoreline of the windward side. As time passed by, both yachts were approaching Cannouan with *National* still in the lead. To Dave's horror and surprise he noticed that *National* intended to pass Cannouan on the windward side. As the sun was about to set, Dave knew that *National* could not possibly clear that treacherous shoreline before total darkness had taken over. When *Margay* closed in on the leeward side of Cannouan, Dave lost sight of *National*, since the island was now between them.

"Turn the radio on," said Dave to his crew. "Put it on frequency 2182. We are going to be listening to a distress call very soon."

The radio had been on for only a few minutes when the call came.

"Mayday, Mayday, Mayday, this is the *National*. A description of their predicament followed. They had run on the reefs on the south east side of Cannouan.

Ring Andersen was anchored in Saline Bay, the south west anchorage of Mayero. We were sharing the bay with only one other visitor, the royal yacht, *Britannia*. I learned of *National's* misfortune when I intercepted a radio conversation between *Margay* and P.S.V. They were discussing the availability of possible craft capable of coming to the rescue. *National* was aground in an area which was surrounded by shallow reefs. The seas were breaking over the coral heads and only a very seaworthy vessel with shallow draft would be able to come close. They did not appear to be able to come up with a likely prospect. I butted into their conversation and suggested that the *Britannia* had large, seagoing, shallow draft launches on board. Perhaps I should ask them for assistance. The idea was worth a try, so I called the *Britannia* on 2182, but without success. No one answered. I put the spot light on the big yacht and tried to arouse some interest that way. Again no luck. The ship appeared deserted and I felt helpless. I was about to climb into the dinghy to bang on the yacht's iron hull, when I heard that in the meantime, Dave Stone had taken matters into his own hands. He had navigated and anchored *Margay* in almost total darkness as close as he dared come to the foundering *National*. This was a feat in itself!

National was firmly embedded on a coral reef and being pounded to pieces. Giant breakers combed her straining decks. Her hull was battered every time a roller exploded against her with enormous force. Each successive wave lifted the ship as it arrived and dropped her onto the sharp coral with an agonizing crash when it passed on. The vessel was breaking up and would not last long. No attempt had been made to try and pull her free. The skipper had locked himself into his stern cabin, which was the only dry place on board. The situation was desperate. The only person who kept her cool and gave comfort to the frightened guests was Marie, the girl from Bequia. She coaxed the group into gathering their valuables and passports, and assured them that help was on its way. David had accomplished the extremely difficult task of anchoring *Margay* in the treacherous area. He launched his inflatable dinghy and with the frail craft, proceeded in amongst the dangerous reefs to get closer to the wreck. Several times he almost capsized and twice he was completely swamped. Miraculously, the outboard motor never missed a beat. For fear of being smashed against the hull of *National* by the turbulent seas, he encouraged the frightened passengers to jump into the water, after which he helped them into the dinghy. He could only take a few at a time. Several trips he made, back and forth and back and forth. In that fashion, he managed to save the entire group of ten passengers and crew.

Dave should have been awarded a medal for his heroic deed, but the charter yachts were not organized at that time, so there was no official group to make that recognition. I still feel, though, that something could have been done if a few boats had gotten together. For lack of better acknowledgement, I dedicate this chapter to our David Stone, who, I was told, has returned to his native New Zealand.

Another person who did an outstanding job during this miserable incident is Marie. She did the job which should have been done by her "gallant " Skipper. Marie courageously assisted Dave with the rescue operation from onboard the foundering hulk.

Bucket

Judy Kwaloff called me from Bequia at ten o'clock on Tuesday morning.

"Jan," Judy said,"your next charter starts in St.Lucia, right?"

"Yes," I answered.

"I wonder if you could do me a favour."

"Sure, Judy, what is it?"

"Bill Dunn has sold my boat, *Bucket*. He has the money and I would like you to bring it with you and put it in my account in St.Lucia."

"You want me to bring up the cheque? Why not just mail it, we won't be in St. Lucia for a couple of days!"

"No, no, it's all cash, in U.S. funds. I don't want it in Bequia because of the foreign exchange rules, and I certainly don't want it transferred via the bank in Grenada because that could turn into an exchange hassle too."

"Oh, I see," I said, now understanding the problem. "O.K., to which bank do I take it and what is your account number, and, eh, how much money is it?" I fumbled for a piece of paper and a pencil to note down the information.

"Seventy six thousand, five hundred dollars."

"What?!"

"Seventy six thousand and five hundred," she repeated. The boat sold for eighty five, and Bill's commission is ten percent."

"Wow! That's a lot of cash to be carrying on board, but I'll see that it gets there. We'll probably be leaving tomorrow, O.K?"

"Thanks, Jan," Judy said. "That's a load off my mind."

After jotting down the account number and the name of the bank, we said goodbye and I hung up the telephone.

I had received the call in the small dock office occupied by the watchman. He didn't have to go far to call me, for the *Ring Andersen* had been moored at her usual berth close to the entrance of the marina. I walked back to the boat and informed Jules of Judy's unusual request. When I told her how much money was involved, she said,"We had better put it into the safe." And jokingly she called after me, as I walked off to see Bill Dunn, "I hope it's big enough!"

Bill Dunn's office is located in the two storey building which houses the Customs office, Patio Bar, shipwright's shop, and machine shop on the main floor. An outside stairway leads to the marina office which is located on the first floor containing a reception area, a charter and sales office to the side, and the manager's office in the back. Bill was shuffling some papers when I entered his domain. I explained the nature of my mission. Apparently, Judy had already advised him how the money would be transported.

"And, you want the money now?" Bill asked.

"Yes, or later today. We'll be leaving early tomorrow morning. Is that a problem?"

"That depends. You can have it as soon as it is dry."

"As soon as it is DRY? What are you talking about?"

"I spent hours this morning pinning it on washing lines in the back garden of my house to let it dry out."

I had heard of laundering money, but this was ridiculous. I sat down in a chair and stared at him in wonder. Noticing my obvious confusion, Bill added,

"Didn't Judy tell you?"

I shook my head, saying, "Tell me what?"

With a sweep of his arm, Bill pushed the papers on his desk aside, sat back in his chair and began to tell me about the sale of *Bucket*, Judy's 'Out Island 41'.

"The boat had been for sale for only a couple of days. I had stuck a for sale sign on her but had not yet advertised her in the usual magazines, when this guy walked into my office and said that he wanted to buy her. I had never seen this fellow before. It turns out he hitched a ride on a yacht which arrived from Trinidad." Bill stood up and pointed through the window at a sailboat moored close to *Bucket*. He sat down again and continued: "The man never quibbled about the price when I told him that the asking price was eighty five thousand U.S. He just said,

"O.K." Bill shrugged his shoulders and paused to polish his spectacles. When finished he put the glasses back on his head and said, "I don't think he actually ever had a good look at the boat. As far as I know, he never went on board— no sea trial— nothing!"

"You must have thought he wasn't really serious, some flake, without money," I suggested.

"Exactly," replied Bill, "That's what I thought too. But then he asked me to go with him to the boat that he had arrived on, to help him get the money. I didn't really understand why he needed my help, but he insisted I come with him, and so I did, why not? When we arrived at the boat he jumped onto the foredeck. There was this stowage locker just forward of the trunk cabin. He opened it and started to pull out these wet, jute bags, some of which he handed to me. I still had no idea what was going on, so I asked him what the bags were for, and he said that the money was in the bags. When I opened one, I noticed it was full of dollar bills."

"You're kidding," I exclaimed amazed.

"No, I'm not," Bill answered, "I've never seen anything like it. We carried the bags to the office, emptied them and started counting, all one dollar bills! It was incredible! There were dollar bills all over the office. On the desk, the chairs, the floor, everywhere! There must have been well over a hundred thousand bills in those bags because when we finally had counted out eighty five thousand, there were still plenty left. And they were all soaking wet from the spray that had come over the foredeck during the trip up from Trinidad, I guess!"

"That is the most amazing story I have ever heard," I uttered in disbelieve. "Where do you suppose he got it?"

"Who knows," Bill replied, shrugging his shoulders. "Drugs, maybe, who knows?"

"Yeah, maybe, but why one dollar bills?"

"I don't know." Bill said, "But anyhow, there you have it, that's what happened. In any event, Judy's boat is sold, but the money is saturated with salt water and it is a bugger to get it dry. I hung some of the bags out to dry and this morning I pinned a whole bunch of bills onto the clothes lines individually. Those should be dry by now, but as for the others, I don't know."

Later on that afternoon, Bill brought five large, brown paper bags containing the entire loot down to the boat. The bags were heavy and damp. There was not enough room for them in the safe, so we stowed them in a closet in the chart room.

In the wee hours of Thursday morning we dropped anchor in the Harbour of Castries, the capital city of St. Lucia. After going through the usual paper work and formalities of clearing customs and immigration, I headed for the bank clutching the money bags in my arms. Arriving at the bank, I went to a side counter and asked to see the manager. In short order he appeared.

"Can I help you?" he asked.

"Yes," I replied. "I would like to make a deposit into the account of Judy Kwaloff."

"Well," he said, "you can do that with any of the clerks at the counter over there." He pointed to the other side of the room were the usual transactions were completed.

"I don't think so," I said, looking around me at the crowd which was gathering in the lineups. I didn't fancy counting out all this money in such public view. Bending over the counter I whispered, "It is a large amount of money; I'd rather not do it there."

Shrugging his shoulders he replied, "Oh, I see, well, then I will get someone for you who will attend to it right here."

"No," I urged, "that won't do either. I want to do this in a private office."

"Hm," he grunted, scratching his head. "That is highly unusual, but if you insist, we can go to my office."

With this he lead the way. As we walked towards his office I chuckled, muttering to myself, "Unusual hey? Well buddy, you're in for a big surprise!"

The bank manager lowered himself into his chair and waved me towards one positioned opposite his desk. Before I sat down, I placed the bags on his desk. As he pulled a deposit sheet out of a drawer, I noticed him throwing an annoyed glance at the brown bags invading the privacy of his desk, probably assuming that they contained the results of a shopping spree.

"Well then," he began, poised with pen and deposit form, "What is the account number and what is the amount?"

I read him the number off the piece of paper I had made the notation on and advised him of the amount.

"Right," he said while filling in the form in precise lettering. "Seventy-six thousand and five hundred U.S. dollars. Will this be by money order or in cash?" he asked while writing.

"In cash," I said while standing up and reaching over, I dumped the contents of one of the bags onto his desk.

His astounded look alternated between the mountain of dollar bills and me.

"But, but, these are all one dollar bills!" he stuttered.

"Yes," I replied, studying his face with mischievous satisfaction. "And the other bags are full of one dollar bills, too!"

With a sigh the poor man started to sort and count out the still damp currency. Several hours later, the task was completed and all the money accounted for. The desk was covered with neat stacks of bills. Looking at my watch, it suddenly occurred to me that it would be too late for me to make it to my own bank to allow me to cash a cheque for the petty cash on board. Looking at the bank manager I said, pulling a cheque book out of my pocket, "Could you cash a cheque for me please? For five hundred dollars U.S.?" I added.

"Do you have an account here?" he asked.

"No, my account is with the Bank of Nova Scotia, a few blocks away from here."

"Well, then I suggest you go there. I can't help you."

"Why not? My bank will be closed by the time I get there and I am leaving St.Lucia this evening."

"You can leave it here on deposit, but I cannot give you any money until it is cleared through your bank."

"For God's sake, don't you trust me? I just brought you all this!" I pointed at the money stacks on the desk.

He shook his head, "Sorry, I can't help you—bank policy!"

I stared at him in disbelieve. Then I grabbed a stack of bills from the desk and said, "O.K., make that deposit an even seventy-six thousand dollars. I am taking five hundred and I will telephone Judy to let her know."

"But," the man exclaimed, "You can't do that! This is not your money!"

"Yes, I can, I just did it!" I replied and wrote out a cheque for five hundred payable to Judy Kwaloff. Handing him the cheque I said, "You can add this to the deposit in lieu of the cash I have taken. That should square things out."

With reluctance he gave me a receipt for the deposit I had made.

What a dork!

Is that you, Jack?

Some of the best seamen can be poor boat handlers. I have seen men repeatedly botch a simple docking manoeuvre, even though they had all the qualifications in the world. Yet, others move a boat around in tight quarters as if playing with a box of matches. Besides experience, good boat handling is an art, which to some comes natural, and to others either with great difficulty or—never!

Jack was one of the unfortunate ones. He had done lots of cruising and was in many ways an old salt, except when it came to docking his forty foot sail boat. The darned thing never seemed to go where Jack wanted to put it. We could all live with this, since Jack's vessel was small enough to fend off. As soon as the alarm of his arrival was sounded, the dock contingency would rush to the various potential points of impact, armed to the teeth with plastic bumpers, to cushion the effect. Those who did not push or shove contributed by shouting instructions, thus confusing the poor bungling skipper even more.

Jack had a dream. He wanted a bigger boat. The boat he fancied was sixty five feet long, and in addition to that had a ten foot bowsprit sticking out over the bow. Jack's dream was lying in one of the marinas in Fort Lauderdale, Florida. The boat was for sale for a very attractive price and Jack decided to not let the opportunity go by. The necessary papers were drawn up, money exchanged hands, and Jack was in possession of his newly found love.

One of the first tasks was to move the boat away from the sales dock to another berth which had been allocated to him by the harbour master. The new berth was behind a fifty-foot Chris Craft, which was in mint condition and sported all the comforts of a modern motor yacht, including a very well appointed aft cabin. The yacht was owned by Jack's British friend, Richard, who was one of those characters who never gets excited over anything and who keeps his cool under any condition.

Jack climbed behind the wheel of his new toy and started the engine. The salesman kindly cast off his lines and walked to the location of the new berth, where he would assist in securing the vessel. Someone else hopped on board to lend Jack a hand. Jack performed exceedingly well. Maybe for some unknown reason, a big boat was more natural to him than a small one. He backed out of the sales slip, executed a perfect 180 degree turn and slowly proceeded to his destination. When he neared the new berth, he altered course slightly to approach at the right angle. He adjusted his course once again to line up parallel to the dock and in so doing, came in for the perfect landing. There was only one problem—Jack was going a wee bit too fast.

"Reverse, Jack!" someone shouted.

"What?" (The engine was noisy.)

"Stop! For Christ sake, stop!"

Jack threw the shift in reverse and opened the throttle. But it is not easy to stop the momentum of some eighty tons of wood and equipment from moving through the water, nor was the fibreglass stern of the motor yacht able to cope with the pressure exerted by the bow sprit of Jack's boat. The wooden spar went through the stern of the fancy cruiser and entered the stern cabin with an agonizing crunch.

Richard, who had been taking a nap in his spacious aft cabin, was thrown out off his bunk by the impact. He fell onto the floor and lay there for a moment gazing at the foreign object that was now firmly embedded into the walls of his cabin and invading a good deal of his private space. He picked himself up from the floor and climbed the stairs to the aft deck. He walked towards the stern and while leaning over the railing, peered down at the new arrival and said, "I say, is that you, Jack?"

Three months later, Richard's boat had been repaired and gone. Jack had not been idle on his dream boat. He had tidied up some odds and ends. He gave the bright work an extra coat of varnish and when all was ship shape, he decided it was time to go for a little trip.

Jack went down the intracoastal waterway

and was having the time of his life chugging down the canal, enjoying his new yacht. When he approached one of the many bridges, he blew the horn to signal the bridge keeper his intention of wanting to pass through.

On the side of the bridges, the State of Florida has installed a sign which displays, with large illuminated numbers, the amount of time remaining to the opening of the bridge. Presumably, this device is activated as soon as a vessel's horn signal is given, because soon after the count down begins.

Jack was familiar with the procedure and also knew that when arriving at the bridge too early, it is a good idea to turn the boat around and if necessary make one or more complete circles, rather than try keeping the boat stationary in the fairly strong current.

As it happened, the device indicated that Jack would reach the bridge well before it was due to open. So, he turned his craft around and proceeded slowly in the opposite direction. Every now and then, he looked over his shoulder at the time display. When he figured the time had come to turn back toward the bridge, he spun the wheel to swing the boat around. But, no luck! The current was playing tricks and would not allow him to complete the turn without running the risk of hitting the boats moored alongside the banks of the canal. Time was running short. The timer continued counting down, 29, 28. Jack was becoming desperate. If he did not make it at this opening, 14, 13, 12, he would have a long wait before the bridge would open again. 8,

7— Jack made a decision. If this boat wouldn't turn around, he would bloody well get through the bridge anyhow. He slammed the gearbox in reverse. Aided by the current, the vessel started to go astern almost immediately. Jack stepped around to the forward side of the steering wheel and, now facing the stern, drove his boat through the bridge backwards. Without incidents and feeling quite proud of himself, he safely reached the other side, much to the amazement of the curious crowd that had gathered to watch this phenomenon from shore. Once more, Jack made an attempt at turning his boat around and this time, success! Happily he continued on his way, this time with the bow pointing into the right direction.

Jack had now almost reached his destination. He was bound for a marina just a bit further along the waterway. The marina had been recommended to him by his friend Richard, who had arranged a berth for him. Not having been in the marina before, Jack approached the entrance cautiously. He spotted one of the marina employees standing on a nearby dock.

"Ahoy there, do you know where my berth is?"

"Yes, it's right over there." The man recognizing the name of the boat as having booked a reservation, pointed to an opening in a row of boats.

"Right, I see it," Jack shouted

"Have you been in here before?" the man queried.

"No."

"O.K. then, it's best to go in there first," he

pointed to the middle of a basin, past the berth. "There you can turn around so that you can go port side to, it's easier with this current. Be careful though, there isn't a whole lot of room!"

Jack entered the basin. He manoeuvred skilfully, considering the limited amount of space. Having completed the 180 degree turn, he steered for his berth. As he came closer, he adjusted his course to line up parallel to the dock. He was coming in for what appeared to be a perfect landing, except— he was going a wee bit too fast.

"Slow down, stop— stop!" someone on the dock shouted.

Jack shifted the gearbox in reverse and opened the throttle, but—too late! With an agonizing crunch, the bowsprit of Jack's craft entered the stern cabin of the motor yacht which was tied alongside the cay.

Richard, who had been asleep in the aft cabin, got knocked out off his bunk by the impact. He rubbed his eyes and stared at the familiar looking bowsprit which was sticking through the bulkhead. "It can't be," he mumbled to himself. With a sigh he stood up, left the cabin and went up onto the aft deck. Leaning over the railing, he peered down at Jack's boat and asked in wonder,

"I say, is that you again, Jack?"

Salvage

Ring Andersen and crew were chartered by General Motors for the making of a commercial type movie. It was filmed for a promotional program whereby dealers were given the choice of a Safari in Africa, a trip to Asia, or a cruise on a charter yacht in the Caribbean. The camera crew who had arrived on board in St. Vincent was to produce a short movie which would give the lucky dealers an idea of what to expect when chartering a yacht.

The film makers had almost completed the footage and were getting ready for the final shot. They had chartered a plane which would take them up in the air for some shots of *Ring* under sail. Timing was critical. We had to be under full sail and in open water when the plane arrived over our heads. For all the time it took for the men to disembark from the boat, climb into the waiting taxi, drive to the airport and board the plane, we had at the most thirty minutes to get ready. As soon as the film crew had left the boat we started preparing for our departure. We were anchored in Kingstown harbour which has very deep water. I had already decided that we would not have time to raise the anchor. Instead, we tied a line with a floating buoy to the bitter end of the chain to mark the spot. We could then retrieve it later. This saved us at least twenty minutes.

We arrived at the designated area at the right time and performed some manoeuvres while the plane was circling overhead. The director of the film crew gave us instructions via radio contact with the pilot. After a while, we were advised that the shoot had been a success and we could return to the anchorage.

Upon returning to Kingstown harbour, we dropped another anchor adjacent to the marker we had left behind and started to pull up on the line to raise the end of the chain. For some reason, the line snapped just as the first links cleared the water. We tried dredging, hoping to hook onto part of the chain, without result. I decided to call the local dive shop which is located at the Mariner's Inn, and asked them to send out a diver. A short while later, two divers with scuba gear arrived. I explained to them what the problem was and where the chain was located. Down they went with another line. In short order the new line was attached to the chain and this time it held. Once the first links were put on the gypsy of the winch, we were home free. Happy with the result I asked the divers how much I owed them. They replied that they did not know, that was for their boss to decide.

We had to leave, because we had to pick up a charter in St. Lucia, so I gave my postal address to the divers and asked them to tell their boss to mail me the bill, but in any event, I would call him at the first opportunity. I thanked them for a job well done and said farewell. After they had been returned to shore, we departed for St.Lucia.

A few days later I called the dive shop from a shore telephone. When the proprietor came to the phone I asked him to tell me what the charges were.

"Yes," he replied, "I figure that anchor and chain is worth about three thousand U.S. dollars,"

"Hold on," I interrupted, "What has that got to do with your bill?"

"Well," he answered, "That was a salvage job, so we base our charges on the value of the salvage."

"You are nuts!" I exclaimed, "It was not salvage. You are talking about my anchor and my chain, which I put down there deliberately. I told your boys where the stuff was located and gave them my line to attach to it. If it was salvage, it was my salvage, not yours! Your divers merely acted upon my instructions."

"No," he said, "we consider it salvage for which we charge fifty percent. You owe me fifteen hundred U.S. dollars."

"Listen buddy," I growled, now getting very annoyed, "I wasn't born yesterday. If you think you are dealing with a scared tourist, you got it all wrong. You sent me two divers. It took them at the most fifteen minutes to tie the line to the chain. That's all they did. We hoisted the thing on board. Including travelling time, they were possibly away from your shop for no more than one hour. You pay those guys probably, at the most, ten dollars

E.C. per hour. I am prepared to pay you sixty dollars U.S. per hour. That comes to one hundred and twenty dollars U.S., take it or leave it. If you accept, I will send you a cheque; if not, you won't get anything until you come to your senses."

"No," he answered, "you owe me fifteen hundred and that's what I want."

"Forget it man. No way! You have my address. Send me a reasonable bill, otherwise no deal!" I hung up the phone.

A few weeks later we were in Grenada. I checked the mail box. There was mail but nothing from the dive shop. We left and went to the Virgin Islands where we operated for several months. When we returned down island some six months later, we anchored off Young Island on a Friday to start a charter on the next day. Young Island is operated as a private resort and is situated only a few hundred feet off the southern shores of St.Vincent. It is a popular anchorage for yachts.

Early Saturday morning I was awakened by a boat banging against our hull sides. I went up on deck to investigate. To my surprise, the gentleman on board the small dinghy which was lying along side, introduced himself as the local sheriff. He presented me with a court order which stated that the *Ring Andersen* was seized and not allowed to leave the anchorage unless I paid the sum of fifteen hundred dollars U.S. plus cost (a substantial amount) forthwith to the dive shop at the Mariner's Inn.

This put us in a terrible position. The new charter was to start today. It was Saturday, the court would be closed. There wouldn't be enough time to argue the claim. It seemed I was completely at the mercy of the scoundrel in the dive shop. I went ashore and managed to locate a lawyer who was willing to see me on his day off. When I explained the situation to him, he suggested I pay the dive shop the amount they had asked for. "After all," he said, "the guy is a poor local fellow who is trying to make a living. You are a rich yacht owner, who can well afford to pay." I got the distinct feeling that I was talking to the wrong guy.

"Not on your life," I said. "In the first place, I'm not a rich yacht owner, and secondly, the man is a crook. I won't be taken for a sucker!"

"Well, in that case," the lawyer shook his learned head, "let me make a call to the Judge."

He called someone, perhaps the judge, perhaps not.

After he put down the phone, he said, "What we can do is this: you give me a cheque for the full amount. The cheque will be deposited in my trust account. I will guarantee the money to the Court which will prove to the Judge that you are acting in good faith. I will act on your behalf to defend your case."

"Will that release my ship?" I asked.

"Yes," he answered, "I can draw up the papers right now."

I felt I was being taken for a ride, but I had no choice. I took out my cheque book and filled in the blanks obediently.

Several times since then, every time we happened to be in St. Vincent, I went to see him and asked how the case was progressing. "When is the hearing? When do we go to court?" Always the same answer,"These things take time. Our courts are very busy."

Eventually, I gave up. I never heard from my lawyer. I wonder how the money was divided. The whole experience has left a sour taste in my mouth for St.Vincent.

The Charter Circuit

The popular charter areas in the Caribbean are the Virgin Islands and the island chain which runs from St.Martin to Grenada. Some boats concentrate on the Virgin Island area which includes the U.S. and the British Virgins. Others specialize on chartering in the other islands which, combined as a group, are referred to as the Leeward and the Windward Islands. Boats chartering the Leewards and Windwards are called Down Island boats. We chartered in both areas, usually down island during the winter and the Virgins in the summer time.

The Virgin Islands encompass a small area and the waters are well protected by the surrounding islands. The Leewards and the Windwards stretch over a much greater distance. The waters between these islands are unprotected and considerably rougher.

Both areas are blessed with the trade winds which steadily blow in from the north east. The wind speed is normally around fifteen to twenty knots, which provides for exhilarating sailing. The temperature ranges in the upper eighty degree mark fairly steadily, winter and summer. Especially on the water, the steady breeze keeps bugs and oppressive heat away. There is no particular rainy season. Rain squalls pass through regularly, but rarely last longer than fifteen minutes.

Squalls, usually packed with an increase in wind speed, can be deceiving.

At one time, when we were en route from St. Lucia to Dominica, the forerunners of hurricane David were battering the area. The wind was brisk, steadily pushing the needle of the wind speed indicator to twenty five knots. We were having a pleasant sail towards Dominica when I noticed a squall line a few miles to starboard of us. The wind speed usually increases drastically during squalls, often by about fifteen knots. I was expecting thirty five to forty knots of wind in the squall. Although *Ring* could handle that amount of wind, it did require extra caution.

I turned on the radar to see where exactly the squall was located and at which point we should go through it. The radar indicated that the squall line was about a mile wide and some four miles long. The long part lay in a south easterly to north westerly direction. Since the prevailing wind would be pushing the squall in a south westerly direction, I reasoned that if we caught the squall as close as possible to its northern point, we would go through the narrow part, or possibly miss it all together. I altered course slightly to the west to meet the selected area. When we entered, the wind was much stronger than I had expected. The wind speed indicator hit fifty plus knots! The worst part was that the wind direction changed completely. The wind in the squall, due to Hurricane David's antics, came from the south east and the squall was travelling in the same direction as we were heading. It meant that we would be travelling the full length of the squall.

Ring shook as she took the full impact of the wind, then she took off like a racing grey hound with a giant bone in her teeth. I put Mankind, alias Rudolph, at the wheel and went forward to keep an eye on things with the crew who stood at the ready for damage control. We were now running before the wind. We sheeted the sails in hard, to spill as much wind as possible and to check the speed of the boat. The sea was rising and I did not want to start falling off the big breakers which were now rolling under us. Reducing sail at this late hour was impossible. We would have to turn into the wind to do this, which meant that momentarily we would get the full force of the wind side ways, which surely would tear our sails to pieces, if not break or rip the masts off the decks.

In the meantime, I kept an eye on the building seas behind us. When one roller suddenly rose high above our stern, I could not help but yell to Mankind, "Hey, Rudolph, look behind you!" Momentarily Rudolph took his eyes off the compass and turned his head. As if having taken sight of the devil, he snapped his head back towards me, his mouth stood open and his eyes were as big as saucers. The whites of his eye balls stood out against the dark skin of his face like the head lights of a vintage Rolls Royce. It was impossible not to laugh at his comical expression. My reaction relaxed Rudolph, who apologetically shrugged his shoulders and turned his attention back to the compass and the steering wheel.

Still charging ahead, with masts and rigging shaking and vibrating and the wind shrieking, *Ring* sped on. We passed Scott's Head at the south western point of Dominica, then the city of Roseau, and finally the tale end of the squall passed us by. We managed to escape without damage. Hurricane David hit Dominica two days later. The destruction to the island was enormous, but by that time we were safely tucked away in Nelson's Dockyard in Antigua.

The west coast of Guadeloupe is protected from the trade winds by a high mountain range. Sailing yachts end up motoring along this coast otherwise they may find themselves adrift for hours on end. Occasional gusts come down the mountains. These gusts are called willywaws, and can be very strong and dangerous, because their direction is downwards instead of horizontal. As a yacht heels by the press of wind into her sails, some of the wind is normally spilled out of the sails as the heel increases. In the case of a willywaw, however, the pressure increases the more the yacht leans over on its side. The cautious sailor takes his sails down or reduces the amount of sail carried when he motor-sails along the Guadeloupe coast line.

We were motoring in a southerly direction along this coast when we spotted a yacht with all sails up passing us by on an opposite course. It was the *Santa Cruz*.

The *Santa Cruz* was a top sail schooner of about eighty feet in length. Before I had the *Ring Andersen*, I looked the *Santa Cruz* over when she was up for sale. She had an interesting history. Originally, she had been a barge built in Argentina and was used in that capacity on the Rio de la Plata. Her hull had subsequently been converted to a pleasure yacht. Whoever had done the conversion had done an excellent job from a pictorial point of view, because the final result was a very handsome looking vessel indeed.

The reasons I had decided not to buy her were the very same reasons she came to her disastrous end. I felt the boat was too narrow in the beam. She felt top-heavy due to her narrow beam, shallow draft and lack of adequate ballast. I considered her rig too tall and her sail compliment too large. All this sums up to an unstable vessel. She would have made a great boat for a movie production, but as far as a sea going vessel is concerned, I did not trust her.

When I declined buying her and made my reasons known to the yacht's owner, he admitted that my opinion was correct. He explained that constantly, he had to make sail changes when wind speeds varied.

Eventually, the yacht was sold to a group of young people who enthusiastically began to make some changes to the yacht's interior to make her suitable for their requirements. I visited frequently with them when they were working on the vessel in Antigua. They were an artistic and talented group who adorned the interior with beautiful wood carvings and exquisite joinery. During one of my visits I impressed upon them my concerns for the vessel's instability and cautioned them to be conservative about the amount of sail they carried.

The sight I was now witnessing, as they were slowly falling behind us, proved that my cautions had fallen upon deaf ears.

A few hours later we heard over the radio that the *Santa Cruz* had been hit by a willywaw and had capsized. Several people went down with the ship.

The Virgin Islands are separated from the Leeward and Windward Islands by the Anegada Passage. This can be a bad stretch of water at the best of times, especially when crossing it in an easterly direction from the Virgins to the Down Island chain. A combination of strong winds and prevailing current can whip up enormous seas.

When the time had come to part company with my treasured *Ring Andersen*, I sold her to a gentleman who could afford to keep her in the manner she deserved. Jules and I stayed on for a while until a new skipper could be found and trained. We were anchored in one of the Virgin Islands and the weather had gone crazy, which is unusual, but periodically it happens. It was blowing so hard that the master of a big freighter had decided to find shelter for his ship by anchoring in the lee of the same island where we were tucked in. A radio call from *Ring Andersen's* new owner informed me of his decision to spend some time in the Caribbean. Could we meet him in Martinique?

"Not likely," I replied into the microphone. "The weather is terrible, too much wind. Also, that generator I had overhauled in St.Thomas is not working properly, I want to take it back to the shop and have them fix it."

"What's that generator worth?" he asked.

"A new one would cost about twelve thousand dollars," I responded.

"Twelve thousand dollars? Then throw the damn thing over the side and buy a new one. I'm not having my holiday plans go haywire for a lousy twelve thousand dollars!"

Hm, I hadn't thought of it that way. I wasn't used to considering twelve thousand bucks as small change.

"There's still the weather," I replied. "There's nothing we can do about that"

"Well, gee, Jan, the *Ring Andersen* is a big boat, I'm sure she can handle a bit of wind— should make great sailing."

Nothing is more difficult than trying to explain to a non sailor that there are times when there is too much wind for a sailing boat, even a boat the size of *Ring*. I tried another approach.

"Why don't you fly to the Virgin Islands and join us here? Then you can enjoy the sail to Martinique as well." I figured that would give us a few more days with the chance that the wind strength had gone back to normal. To this he agreed.

Two days later, the new boss arrived. The wind had not abated and the seas, which could be seen from a high vantage point on the island, had grown bigger! I tried to explain that it would be lunacy to go out in that kind of weather. I could see his reaction of disappointment on each of the following mornings when I had to refuse to raise the anchor. I felt bad about this because it obviously didn't make him a very happy camper. When on the third day I was about to repeat the same message, a thought suddenly occurred to me. I realized that this man had no idea what it would be like to be out in a boat in this kind of weather. Surely, if we went out for a short spin, the experience was bound to shake the pants off him, in which case we could turn back to the anchorage and I wouldn't have to deal with the problem anymore. When he appeared for breakfast and popped the usual question, I answered in the affirmative.

Happily, he watched us prepare for the departure. Being a good sport, he pitched in with enthusiasm. The engine was started, the anchor winched on board, and the sails were raised. After leaving the anchorage, I stopped the engine and we poked our noses outside. It was bedlam. The wind howled, the yacht pitched, and breaking seas belted the hull and decks. For those on deck, both hands, arms and other limbs were needed to hold onto whatever was closest. I watched our new owner groping around the deck, trying to find a secure hold to prevent him from loosing his balance. My plan had not worked! To my amazement, he had a big smile on his face and shouted to me that he was loving every minute of it! His appetite was not effected either, because during lunch time, he dug in with enthusiasm. We were committed. Come hell or high water, Martinique or bust!

We were sailing under reefed sails. I could not reduce the area too much since we needed the driving power to be able to force on through the big seas. The first thing that went wrong was the coming on board of a big sea that came from the port side, went over the deckhouse and slammed into the shore boat which was hanging on the starboard davits. It carried the boat away, tore off one of the davits and along with it, ripped some fifteen feet of our starboard bulwarks planking clear of the stanchion posts. The shore boat, still attached by one of its cables and now being towed along side, was slamming into the hull. With all hands available we managed to haul the boat back on board and clear away the remaining debris. A few hours later the mainsail snapped with a loud crack. It tore horizontally along one of the seams. Again, it took all hands to get the remains down and off the mast and boom. We were now sailing with forestaysail and mizzen alone. The boat slowed down and I did not like the pitching motion. She was slow and sluggish in response to the helm. I decided to call for additional sail area. We raised one of the jibs, but it soon tore to shreds and had to be taken down again. Jules cried out that there was trouble inside the boat. The book case which was bolted to a bulkhead in our cabin had come crashing down. It didn't matter, was not important. We left the pieces lying where they had fallen. The engine was started, and with the propeller turning, we picked up extra speed. This improved the steering capability and kept the yacht on course. We were now motor sailing. Slowly we clicked off the miles in the direction of our destination. The wind shrieked, the seas building up with the crests being blown off the tops. Every now and then we would encounter an even bigger wave. *Ring* would labour over it, lift her stern clear out of the water and then bury her bows into the next one. Each time the stern lifted, the propeller came out off the water and sped up. Ba ba ba ba—a quick succession of vibrations as the prop and engine accelerated, the vibration felt throughout the ship. Eventually, this caused the shaft log, which is the aperture through which the propeller shaft exits the hull, to shake loose. Water started to come in. We now had to start the pumps every twenty minutes. The ship's cat panicked as it was washed towards the missing boards of the bulwarks. With a giant and heroic leap, Jules managed to scoop it up, just before it was about to disappear over the side. The staysail ripped to pieces. We cleared away the remains and lowered the mizzen sail and hoisted it where the mainsail had been. This was no small feat, but it had to be done to get better balance. The sail acted as a steadying sail to prevent us from rolling in great arcs.

Eventually, we managed to claw ourselves towards the lee of St.Kitts, where we dropped anchor to make repairs. Also in the anchorage was a large motor yacht owned by a wealthy Arab. I knew her skipper, Peter Lee. While taking a breather from straightening out the mess on board, which included sorting out the library which was in chaos, I called Peter on the radio.

"What are you doing here?" I asked.

"Same thing you are," he answered, "making repairs!"

To the new owner it had been an exciting experience, very much enjoyed. I was glad we were safely anchored and still afloat!

Many of the down island boats charter in the Mediterranean during the summer and in the Caribbean during the winter. Some would go north, to the east coast of the United States for the summer, and some would, every once in a while, make a world circumnavigation to make things more interesting.

I would guess, it is fair to say, that all charter skippers have put a lot of blue water miles under their keels. Most have made several ocean crossings and quite a few have done one or more circum-navigations.

Whereas in cosmopolitan areas, where boating is done purely for pleasure, one talks of going offshore and treats it with much deference, in the Caribbean community, the term offshore does not exist. Virtually all charter work is offshore. In North American marinas, the yachtsman who has just completed an offshore passage is looked upon as somewhat of a hero. In charter circles, he is no different from anyone else. This phenomenon is sometimes not understood by the cruising yachtsman who has just completed his first Atlantic crossing and arrives in the islands from Europe.

He ties his boat up, walks over to the local bar, be it Grenada or Antigua, and spots a bunch of yachties involved in a card game.

"Hi, I am Dick Smith," and he adds expectantly, "I've just crossed the Atlantic from England!"

The response he is likely to get goes something like this.

"Oh, hi, Dick, nice to meet you. Go and get yourself a beer and sit down."

The others will probably mumble an equal, hi or hello, and then the card game will carry on without further interruption.

Some cruising sailors are really put off by this phlegmatic reply and think that they are made unwelcome. This, however, is not so. The reason that their arrival is treated without fanfare is that probably everyone in the circle has made the trip so many times that the new arrival's feat makes very little impression.

Some cruising sailors support their travels by writing articles about their adventures, and I enjoy reading their published works. On occasion, however, I have noticed that some have little good to say about the people involved in the charter industry. Some of this animosity no doubt comes from what they feel is a cool reception in the islands by the charter fraternity. It's not that they are received coolly, they are just not treated with the same heroism they would have been treated with at the yacht club of their home port.

I recently read an account of a voyage by a fellow whose books have been widely published and who has the talent of telling his stories with great excitement. He must have experienced a simular situation, because some of the things he said about the charter business and the people in it are malicious and grossly exaggerated. I suspect that his pride was hurt when he was not treated as the famous globetrotter he felt he was. This same fellow boasts about having crossed the Atlantic sixteen times. That's a lot of crossings for a yachtsman, but many charter skippers have made that crossing twice as often. I know of one such charter captain who sailed to England and back because he wanted to be home for his daughter's birthday. He stayed in the U.K. for one weekend and then returned to the West Indies to complete his charter schedule.

Don Street, also known as Squeaky, on a moment's whim, drove his old boat, *Iolaire*, without engine, all the way to England and back, because he felt like participating in the Fastnet race. He raced her, too. Wearing his tattered old straw hat, I understand Don caused quite a lot of consternation amongst the la-di-da racing fleet.

Don related to me that when he was battling for a good position at the starting line with a very sleek racing yacht and apparently winning, the skipper of the racing yacht took a closer look at the *Iolaire*—Don Street apparition and yelled, "Only those boats racing are allowed to fly the racing flag."

Upon which Don shouted back, "What the hell do you think I'm doing, riding a bicycle?"

A husband and wife team, Hans and Erica, who owned the converted 12 metre yacht *Flica*, thought it quite normal to sail 1200 miles or so to New York to go on a shopping spree or pick up some parts, true to their slogan "It's Quicka by Flica!"

I gather that the famous author and globe trotter, who I referred to earlier, makes some derogatory comments about the *Ring Andersen* in one of his books, although he does not mention our boat by name. He refers to charter yacht owners who are exploiting the local black people. Through an incident which occurred in Tortola, it became obvious that his comments were directed at us.

Ring Andersen's usual berth in the Village Cay Marina at Road Town, Tortola, was at the very end of one of the fingers of the dock. This was the only berth large enough to accommodate the yacht. Village Cay Marina was one of the newer establishments in Road Town and included a modest hotel and two restaurants. The operation was very capably managed by its creator, John Ackland, who we had become quite fond of. At the head of the marina, along the shore side, was a building which amongst other facilities, accommodated the two restaurants, one trés chic, located upstairs, and another one, designed mainly for the lunch crowd, situated downstairs. The establishment was appropriately called the 'Upstairs Downstairs'.

My wife Jules and I were having lunch at the Downstairs when we suddenly spotted our crew coming towards us from the end of the dock where the *Ring Andersen* was tied up. They moved on past us in the typical West Indian way, swaying in rhythm to a tune audible through a small radio carried by Steam Box. I don't know if I have yet mentioned that these guys were all impressive in size and well muscled. After passing the restaurant, they made a turn and disappeared up the other finger of the dock. For a moment, both Jules and I wondered what was going on, but then paid no further attention when the waiter distracted us to take our order. About twenty minutes later, we observed the guys coming back from the other dock, passing the restaurant again and then returning to *Ring*. The radio was still playing and the walk was, as usual, reggae in sync with the rhythm.

A few minutes later an irate, newly hired assistant manager confronted us at our table. John Ackland was away on a business trip and the new man left in charge was obviously under great stress.

"Are you the owners of the *Ring Andersen*?" he demanded to know.

"Yes," I said. "Is there a problem?"

"You bet there is," he fumed. "Your crew just beat up the crew of another yacht. I want you to know that I won't tolerate this type of behaviour. I'm going to tell your crew right now that they are not to leave the boat, and if they don't obey my order then I want your boat out of here immediately!" The man stood there shaking with agitation.

"Calm down," I said. "In the first place, there must be an explanation for this. My crew doesn't go around beating up on people without very good reason, and secondly, you stay away from my boat and my crew. My crew only takes orders from me."

"Well, eh, well," he stammered, "I can not tolerate this!"

"I know," I replied, "you already said that. Take it easy! I'll find out what is going on." With this, I stood up and walked towards *Ring*.

When I arrived at the boat I saw the crew busily engaged with the end for end turning of one of the forestaysail sheets. When I approached the area were they where working, they pretended to be too busy to notice me.

"Alright," I said, "what's been going on?"

They looked up from their task with innocent faces.

"What you mean, Skip?" enquired J.P.

The others sniggered and pretended some new found interest in the condition of one of the blocks through which the forestaysail sheet was led.

"Come on, guys," I said, "the new assistant manager of the marina is so upset that his blood vessels are about to burst. What the heck have you fellows been up to?"

"Well, Skip, nothing much happened. We just had a little talk with a the crew from another boat," Vibert volunteered.

"Oh, and what exactly do you mean by a little talk?" I enquired. "The fellow of the marina tells me a different story."

Then, in bits and pieces, I learned the details of the story.

It turned out that the well known author's boat had been anchored close to us in the anchorage a few days ago, in the harbour of Charlotte Amalie, the main city of St.Thomas. Apparently, the author had amongst his crew a hand who was a native from Dominica. This fellow, on several occasions, had shouted remarks to my crew and accused them that they were Uncle Toms and were working on a slave ship. The man was obviously influenced by his boss, the author, since similar comments are made in his written pages. At first, my crew did not give the insults much attention, although I can well imagine that they were angry because they were as proud of *Ring Andersen* as I was.

I had listened to their report with great interest.

"I see," I said, and encouraging them to continue I asked, "and then what happened?"

"Well, Skip," Vibert answered, "our boat's no slave ship and we're no Uncle Toms. We like working on *Ring Andersen* and we like working with you!"

"Yes," Thomas added, "you treat us good, Skip! You're no slave driver, you're our Skip." This comment was affirmed with the nodding heads of the others who had now gathered around me.

"So, what happened here?" I asked, choking a little on this piece of loyalty.

"The boat—that boat," Vibert corrected, meaning the author's boat, "passed by us a little while ago and tied up to the dock over there." He pointed to the approximate vicinity where the yacht was located. "When they passed by us, real close, they yelled at us again, calling us names and yelling, slave ship, slave ship!"

"Ah," I said, beginning to understand the situation. "And after that, you guys went over there, and that is when Jules and I saw you pass by the restaurant."

"Yes, Skip," said Thomas. "We just sorted them out a little; there'll be no more problems."

"I guess not," I commented, suppressing a laugh with great difficulty.

I returned to the restaurant where I informed the Assistant Manager that the situation was under control and that there was no need to worry about the peace in the Marina. In Thomas' words, 'There'll be no more problems'.

It has been said that chartering is a rat race. Well, in a way it is. Probably anything that one does because it has to be done, is a rat race of some sorts. Living in a city, keeping up with the Joneses in a nine to five job is a rat race. The business entrepreneur, who makes millions, lives in a rat race. Meeting a heavy charter schedule, getting the boat ready on time is a rat race. But cruising and getting the sails down before a squall, or having to make entries in the log, keeping track of the course and having to make a position fix, could be called a rat race. Writing a story and meeting the publisher's deadline is a rat race. Take your pick, which one do you prefer? That's what it's all about. Some rat races are enjoyable, others are not.

Chartering is business. Cruising is fun time off. The advantage of chartering is, that one gets to do both, sometimes at the same time. Most charters I have enjoyed so much and the guests were such pleasant company, that I might as well have been cruising for my own pleasure.

A business is supposed to make a profit. In the normal world, profits are judged by monetary gain. The charter business does not work that way. From a monetary point of view, chartering is a complete flop. This point may be argued by many charter operators, but their accountants would agree with me. If one considers the interest involved in the investment, the depreciation, wear and tear and the hours of labour, any accountant would concur that from a business point of view chartering is insane. At the time of this writing, *Ring Andersen*, which is in the luxury charter trade, charges $18,000.00 per week for a party of six people. If the yacht does about sixteen charters she will just about pay for her keep, but this does not include wear and tear, depreciation, and unforeseen expenditures. There is another way of looking at it. During one of the general meetings of the Caribbean Charter Yacht Association, we discussed the subject of charter rates and the related problems of profit and loss. Soon it became evident that the opinions of what was a profitably operating yacht varied widely. We all agreed to one thing though, if there was enough money to keep the boat in first class condition, we were all happy. A voice rang out from the discussion group.

"You guys have got it all wrong."

The speaker was Helen Reed. She and her husband, Bob, owned and ran the yacht *Eudroma*. Helen was a vivacious, petite, suntanned blond and very attractive lady. She was also extremely enthusiastic about chartering.

"We all make good money chartering," she exclaimed as she rose from her seat to make her point.

"Only very wealthy people can live the lifestyle that we live. Bob and I would have to have a net annual income of at least sixty thousand dollars in order to be able to cruise these islands on a yacht year after year. So, as far as I am concerned, we make a net profit of sixty thousand each year!"

Having said that, she looked around the group of yachties, waiting for a challenge to her statement. When none came, she sat down with a triumphant smile. Helen was right! Our business was not about money, it was about supporting a lifestyle we all enjoyed!

Down, But Not For The Count

They say everyone is entitled to make one mistake. I have made several. Lack of foresight and total miscalculation of time needed for repairs once put us in a very awkward position.

One of the dangers of success in the charter business is too much repeat business. This sounds crazy, but it is true. If all previous customers keep repeating, it is possible to land in a situation where the entire schedule is booked with return clients. This is bad. One needs new blood, so to speak, to balance the season. The reason is this. People will keep coming back to the same area only so many times. They will return twice, thrice, maybe four times, but then they want to see something clse. If a boat is filled up every available week with guests who have made the trip too many times, the next season one might be sitting with an empty calendar.

It is also possible to charter too many weeks in the year. In this case the hours for necessary maintenance are cut short, the yacht suffers and eventually demands her deserved time in double instalments.

We had fallen foul of both obstacles. We had

completed a year of thirty two weeks of charter work. Over eighty percent had been repeat customers. The majority of these had been on *Ring* many times before. I knew most of them would not come back to the Caribbean. Because of the heavy charter schedule, we had fallen behind with maintenance. Also, I had now earned enough money to do something I had wanted to do for a long time.

Ring Andersen's capping rail was not in the best of conditions. It had been repaired many times by fitting in small pieces, in the trade called Dutchmen, presumably because it is a cheap and quick way to make repairs. I wanted to replace the entire rail with new teak. *Ring's'* capping rail was ten inches wide and three inches thick. There was quite a bit of money involved. I also figured if we wanted our customers to return, we had better offer them a change of scenery. Thus, the decision was made to go to the Mediterranean after the refit.

The work on *Ring* started, and in the meantime we advised our charter brokers and clientele that we were going to Greece and would not be available in the Caribbean that year. Soon the bookings started to come in and we looked forward to a successful charter season in Greece.

Ring's refit progressed more slowly than anticipated. When the capping rail was removed, it was decided to replace some of the wooden stanchions or bulwark frames. To replace these frames, it was also necessary to replace the bulwark planking. Anyone who owns a boat, especially a wooden boat, knows of this procedure. Once you start tearing away, it's difficult to stop. Before long, it became apparent that we would not be able to finish the job in time for the long haul to Greece. The necessary wheels were set in motion to advise our charter guests and persuade them to join us in the Balearic Islands instead. Some said, "Yes," but some said, "No." So, we lost some bookings.

Then I made my biggest boo-boo. I received an invitation from the Tall Ships Society to take *Ring* to Vancouver for the celebration of Captain Cook's discovery of Nootka Sound.

My heart jumped a few beats as I read the letter. The thought of entering *Ring* in the Tall Ships Race and taking part in the celebrations got my blood pumping with excitement. My mind raced. *How can I do it and cover the costs? Maybe,* I thought, *I can get our charter guests to spend the summer in the Pacific Northwest. Then, in the fall we have to go back to the West Indies, to be there in time for the winter charter season. If I can get enough bookings in British Columbia, I might be able to swing it.*

On and on, my thoughts dealt with the problem. We contacted our charter clients again and asked if they would be interested in going to British Columbia instead of the Balearic Islands?

The same response as before. Some were and some were not. By now we had very few bookings left. Reality caught up with me. We would not be able to make it. With all the fooling around and changing the route repeatedly, people had started to make other plans. They must have thought that I was fickle. And rightly so!

The final upshot of this scenario was that after the refit was finally completed, we were still in the Caribbean, we had no bookings, and the charter agents had no idea where we were, or where we were going. We ended up taking *Ring* to the Virgin Islands in search of business. Hopefully we would pick up some last minute bookings.

Some time later, we were anchored in the Bight, an anchorage at Norman Island in the British Virgins. *Ring* lay there in all her splendour, paint shining, bright work gleaming and her varnished spars reaching towards the sky.

The anchorage was a favourite for the Bare Boats, so called because they can be rented or chartered without crew. As usual, *Ring's* beautiful hull and impressive size attracted a lot of attention. Often, the bare boaters came out in their dinghy, circling the yacht, to admire her from every angle. As they stared at *Ring*, they would shout comments to each other. The reason they shouted, was to be heard over the noise created by the outboard motor which was propelling their dinghy. But, sound and water have a strange way of reacting together. While the people in the dinghy had to shout at each other to be heard, unbeknownst to them, they were clearly audible fifty feet away to those on board the *Ring Andersen.*

It was one of those eavesdropping sessions which gave me an idea that helped us out of a very uncomfortable situation.

Ring's running expenses and the cost of the last refit, including the new bulwarks, had eaten heavily into the ship's purse. Because of my fickle management we had no charters booked or to look forward to in the near future. Our financial situation was downright desperate. We had exactly one dollar left in the kitty!

While the oglers were feasting on *Ring Andersen's* appearance, I was inside the saloon racking my brains over a possible solution to the problem. I could think of none!

My train of thought was interrupted by the sound of a boat going by. I stood up, walked to the saloon door which led onto the deck, opened it and took a look outside. I noticed one of the bare boats passing us at a distance of about eighty feet. The boat was motoring out of the anchorage. In the cockpit by the wheel sat a lady who was peering through binoculars. She steadied them to her eyes by leaning on the cockpit coaming with her elbows. The binoculars were aimed at us. Other people seated in the cockpit were also looking towards us. On the fore deck of the yacht were two men. They were making preparations to hoist the sails, but while busy with their task, they were looking in our direction as well. Suddenly, I heard the woman with the binoculars shout to the men,

"Hey, look at that, they have a launch on the other side too!"

It seemed she was referring to our shore boats which were suspended from davits on either side of the deck house. One of the men on the foredeck boomed back at her with a heavy New Jersey accent, "Yeah, some rich f***er owns that son of a—"

Obviously, our entire crew had overheard the exchange, because an instant howl of laughter reverberated along *Ring's* decks. I was laughing so hard that I had to hold my aching stomach with one hand while steadying myself against the deckhouse door-frame with the other. A look across the deck showed the crew in equal discomfort. The tears were rolling down their faces. I stumbled back into the saloon and let myself fall into one of the chairs to recuperate.

The entire episode had been missed by Jules and Michele who had been below, reading. Alerted by the noise, they now came up the stairs and entered the saloon where I was still sitting in the chair, wiping the tears from my face.

"What was that all about?" asked Jules. "Did we miss something?"

"You sure did," I answered, still laughing, and filled them in on what had happened. When the scene had been re-enacted and Michele had gone on deck to get another version from the crew, both Jules and I pondered the irony of the incident, the, 'so called rich owner' versus the one, lonesome dollar in our piggy bank. The anti climax caused us both to fall quiet, each to our own thoughts. After a few moments, a tiny light began to twinkle in my brain. It slowly started to spread its glow. As the light brightened, I got up from my chair and started to pace back and forth. Thinking out loud, not expecting an answer, I said, "I wonder just how interested all those bare boaters are in *Ring* ?"

"What do you mean?" Jules queried.

"I am thinking about them having a vacation in those boats without crew. The men have all the fun, sailing and playing with the boat, but what about their wives?"

Perplexed, Jules looked at me and answered, "Mostly, they are below cooking and cleaning, they are slaving away, waiting on their husbands, just as they do at home!"

"Right," I replied. The light in my head was now burning at full capacity. "And I bet they would just love to have their husbands take them out—"

"To a nice candlelight dinner on *Ring Andersen*!" Jules completed.

"Exactly!" I said.

Jules went rapidly into high gear. With a piece of paper and a pencil, she sat down at the table and started making notes.

"A steak dinner would probably be best," I heard her mutter as she was thinking out loud.

I left her to it. Jules had been trained in hotel management in England. She had been assistant manager of a posh resort in the Caribbean, and managed a restaurant in Gibraltar and Cyprus. Working out the details of our new brain wave was right up her alley.

I went in search of my drawing pens. After finding them, I wrote invitations for a sumptuous dinner by candlelight on board the yacht *Ring Andersen*. I completed this with a sample of the menu that Jules had planned. I proceeded to make several copies. We then weighed anchor and departed for nearby Road Town to stock up on supplies. Fortunately, we could buy these on credit from our regular suppliers.

The same day we returned to the Bight. By 3:00 PM we dropped the hook in the middle of the anchored bare boat fleet. As soon as the boat was securely anchored we lowered the shore boats and had the crew distribute the invitations to the boats in the anchorage. I stood by the radio to take reservations. They started to come in even before our shore boats had returned. Success! We had a full house.

Jules and Twin were cooking in the galley. The steward waited on the table. I performed as maitre'd and one of the crew was bartender on the aft deck, where waiting groups enjoyed cocktails. The rest of the crew were frantically washing dishes on the foredeck since the galley was too crowded. The dirty plates and cutlery were pushed through the port holes where they were grabbed and passed on to the scrubbing foredeck hands. The whole thing operated as smoothly as an assembly line in a Japanese factory.

This little caper got us started in the floating restaurant business which allowed us some breathing time to look for charters.

During one of our brief visits to Road Town, Tortola, where we now regularly replenished our stores for the candlelight dinners, a young lady stopped by our boat and asked to speak to the captain. When I approached her, she introduced herself and stated the reason for her presence. She said that she had been admiring the *Ring Andersen* and was about to be married. When the puzzled look on my face obviously indicated my missing the connection between her getting married and her admiration for *Ring*, she continued by explaining that she would like to get married on board! Could she charter *Ring* for her big day, and could we cater to her wedding? I of course said, "Yes," and in my enthusiasm said that I would even perform the ceremony. She laughed at this and replied that that was not necessary. The ceremony was already arranged, but she would like to have the reception, which was to take place afterwards, on board. She then told me that she lived in Panama and was marrying the accountant of the Caneel Bay Plantation, one of the most attractive, Laurance Rockefeller, resort hotels in the islands. We only needed to provide the boat and crew, the resort would look after everything else. To me, this sounded even better, because it meant that we did not even have to provide food and drinks for who knows how many people. I made a quick calculation and quoted her two thousand dollars, which at that time was a fair bit of change, but *Ring* was well worth it. She immediately agreed.

Later that day she came by with her parents who signed the charter contract and paid the fee. We discussed the details of the reception which was to take place a few days later.

The Caneel Bay Plantation is situated in Caneel Bay on the island of St. Johns. We were to anchor in the Bay at noon to allow the hotel staff to prepare the ship for the reception. Food, dishes and cutlery had to be brought on board and also a certain amount of festive decorating would be done at that time. The reception would begin at about 5:00 PM, at which time we would start ferrying people on board. Once everyone was on board, we would go out for a short cruise to arrive back at the anchorage in the Bay later that evening. We could expect about eighty people, plus a band of musicians and the hotel catering staff.

On D day, we dropped the anchor at 1200 hours sharp at the designated spot. We then witnessed a well oiled machine going to work. In no time flat, the boat was decorated with balloons and other appropriate decorations. Lights were rigged on the deck area between the deck house and the steering station. The band was to take up position here and the remaining area provided space for a dance floor. Then the saloon and saloon table were decorated with flowers. Last, sumptuous food was brought in. Along with the food came the centre piece, a beautiful butter sculpture. How this remained standing without melting in the tropical heat remains a mystery to me to this day. The whole thing was organized by the assistant manager of the resort. It was awesome to see this pro and well-trained staff at work. Everything was so smooth and well planned and above all, all of the staff were in the best of spirits, happy faces, courteous and friendly.

The boat was ready well in time for the guests to arrive, some of whom we picked up with our shore boats, while others were delivered by the hotel staff who operated boats owned by the Resort. Shortly before dark we hoisted the anchor and got underway.

We slowly motored out of the bay. We had a lot of people on board. We stopped counting when the number reached one hundred and twenty. I decided to not raise sails. It would be impossible with this number of bodies; someone might get hurt when in the way of a block, or trip over a line. So, we kept on motoring. We negotiated the narrow Durloe passage between Hawksnest Point and two small off-lying islets and then moved on to Francis Bay, where we anchored while some speeches were delivered to the newlyweds by some of the friends and family. During the return trip the spirits of the party goers became more and more festive. The band was playing and the dance floor was packed with moving bodies. It was now pitch dark. Whereas normally the stars illuminated the area surrounding *Ring*, allowing me some visibility in way of being able to tell the difference between water and land, the lights suspended over the dancing crowd directly ahead of me almost completely blinded my vision. As long as we were in a reasonably wide stretch of water I could cope with the problem, but I was worried about the narrow passage we had to negotiate before being able to enter Caneel Bay. Jules and I discussed the problem. The simple answer was to turn off the lights and ask the band to stop playing when we entered the passage. But this might put a damper on the good time enjoyed by the crowd. We decided to go in on radar. The fact that the radar was located in the chart room which is situated in the port aft section of the saloon, and therefore not visible from the steering station, was solved by Jules standing in the doorway with her eyes on the radar, and myself watching Jules who would give me hand signals over the crowd. Pointing to the left for a little to port, pointing to the right for a little to starboard, or straight up for steady as she goes. We decided to give it a short test run. It worked beautifully! Soon we entered the narrow passage.

I kept my eyes trained on Jules who guided me in. So far so good, slowly we crept on. I could not slow down too much because there is some current here. To keep good steerage I needed to keep some speed up, about 3 knots. Almost half way there! Suddenly, I noticed Jules' hand wave erratically, next, she was by my side.

"The radar went out. The thing is on the blink," she said.

"Great," I grunted, "what perfect timing."

"Shall I turn the lights off, or can you stop?"

"No," I answered, "I can't stop. Too much current and it's too late to turn the lights off, just keep your fingers crossed."

I peered through the darkness trying to shade my eyes against the lights suspended over the crowd. I actually felt, more than saw, the presence of land slowly pass by the sides of the boat. The passage is only about 1500 feet long but it felt more like several miles. During what seemed like an eternity, but was in fact only minutes later, we finally could see the welcoming lights of the resort as we rounded the point, allowing us to safely slip into the welcoming bay. With a sigh of relief I gave the signal to drop the anchor.

The party lasted well into the night. Most definitely, a good time was had by all. Some days later we received a thank you note from the happy couple. Enclosed were pictures of what they thought had been the best wedding ever!

A few days later, we booked a three week charter which took us back to the Windward Islands. We were back in the charter business!

The Phantom Bareboat

Times are a changing and so is the charter scene. The big yachts with their full complement of crew, offering charters with all the luxurious trimmings, are slowly being replaced by the bareboat industry. It is not only a matter of money. Today's traveller is becoming more and more interested in active holidays. Rather then sitting on a beach or lazing around on a big yacht while being pampered by service personnel, people are now into doing things—hiking, skiing, safaris, sailing. Travel companies offer backpack tours, trapping tours, scuba diving vacations, white water rafting, survival trips, etc. All these types of activities are gradually becoming the fashionable and popular thing to do. Perhaps it is because people are becoming more health conscious, or a different type of stress relief is needed from the increasing pressures of daily life.

The bareboat answers this call of participation. A bareboat can be rented, without crew, with or without provisions, and is operated by the vacationer. The charterer does the planning, the cooking, navigating, and handling of the boat. Companies offering this kind of service have been springing up all over the world in those areas where boating is a popular pastime. Organizations such as Caribbean Yacht Charters, Sea Breeze Charters, Barefoot Yacht Charters, and The Moorings, to name a few, have established large fleets of boats in prime areas throughout the world. Their boats are of newish vintage, maintained by a skilled staff, and they offer emergency services throughout the charter area for assistance in case of break down. Those who use their services are required to provide proof of their capabilities to operate the craft and are given a briefing before setting off on their cruise. Through this facility, yachtsmen now have the opportunity to sail in other areas of the world without having to relocate their own craft, or better yet, forego the expense of owning a boat altogether and still being able to have a yachting vacation in an area of their choice. Considering the many advantages, it is no wonder that the bareboat idea has become extremely popular.

Whereas in the late sixties and early seventies we would share an anchorage with mainly large, fully crewed charter yachts and some cruising sailors, as time goes on, the anchorages are now mostly occupied by bareboats.

The bareboat industry has intrigued me because one would expect that since the occupants of the boats are generally weekend sailors and unfamiliar with the area, this would lead to accidents and disaster. Yet, this is rarely the case. I suppose that the screening process, the good overall condition of the boats and the back up system provided by the bareboat company is responsible for the low accident rate.

If any criticism is due to the bareboaters it is probably their lack of skill in anchoring. Most likely this is because of the fact that when operating in their home waters they move from marina to marina, allowing them to tie up to a dock, rather then having to anchor out in a bay or cove. Often, their desperate antics in getting the anchor to hold, were observed by us and our guests with some amusement. Often, a bareboat was seen approaching the anchorage, the anchor and tackle seen to be cast overboard, the helmsman backing up the boat to set it and going backwards and backwards and backwards, until the craft had nearly disappeared from sight. Then the equipment would be retrieved, the boat would come back, this time trying a slightly different spot, only to start the whole process once again. Frequently, this procedure would be repeated again and again. On occasion an argument would erupt on the bareboat, the watch would change in that the helmsman and the person standing ready at the anchor would change places, like, "I'll show you how to do this," usually to the spectator's enjoyment and with no better results.

The *Ring Andersen* was anchored in Gorda Sound near the resort, The Bitter End. The anchorage is popular because of its scenery, beaches, protection from the trade winds and most of all, the resort, which welcomed weary sailors to excellent drinks and dinner served in a first class restaurant. We were anchored well back in the bay and shared the anchorage with numerous crafts of the bareboat variety.

At about five o'clock in the afternoon, just before darkness set in, and when most bareboaters had gone ashore for dinner, we saw two bareboats coming towards us. The first boat was closely followed by the second which was of identical make and size. When the boats came closer to us I noticed that the helmsman of the first boat repeatedly looked over his shoulder toward his pursuer. He seemed to be distraught. His companions appeared to be excited and also had their eyes trained on the boat which was following. When they were closer to *Ring*, I saw that the second boat had no one at the wheel, in fact, no one was to be seen on board. In short order our entire crew and passenger complement had now become aware that something unusual was going on. Obviously, the frantic skipper tried to get away from the boat which was following him. He abruptly changed his course a few times to get out of the way of the pursuer, but to no avail. The other boat turned with each course change too. I noticed that the first boat did not have its anchor on board. When I looked at the bow of the second boat I saw that its anchor was missing as well.. A rope stretched from the bow forward into the water. Suddenly, the whole situation became clear to me. By now, both boats were very near to us and would pass close to our port side. The bareboat skipper saw his chance. He figured he could trick his pursuer by going past us and then doubling back on his course by going around our stern. I yelled at him as he came within ten feet of *Ring's* stern.

"Stop! The other boat's anchor is caught in yours! You can't escape if you keep going!"

Up to that moment the man had been concentrating so much on his predicament that he had not noticed the audience which had gathered on the aft deck of the *Ring Andersen.* He looked at me with a desperate expression in his face.

"What shall I do?" he implored despairingly.

"Slowly come alongside us, we will help you tie up."

In the mean time, our crew had fended off and grabbed hold of the second boat which had threatened to bang into our port side. The man did as I had asked. Slowly he manoeuvred his boat along side. We now had one bareboat tied to starboard and another to port. The anchor lines and chain were under our keel connecting the two boats from port to starboard. While the frantic skipper and his companions were recuperating onboard the *Ring* with a couple of stiff drinks, it took my crew and I close to an hour to sort out the mess. With both anchors safely stored on board both vessels, boat number one, including her now happy and high spirited party, left to re-anchor a safe distance away from us. We could hear them singing well into the hours of the evening.

In the mean time, the other boat was still tied along side. I decided to anchor her well behind us. With one of the shore boats we towed her to a spot about a hundred feet beyond our stern and set her anchor. When back on board, Jules and my charter guests, who had been playing host to the now departed bareboaters, filled me in on the activities which had led to the chase. Apparently, boat number one had started to drag anchor. When they tried to heave their anchor back on board they couldn't lift it because it was too heavy. The skipper then decided to leave whatever was left remaining of the ground tackle in the water and drag the whole shebang to another place in the anchorage. He had not realized however, that his anchor had dragged into the anchor set out by the other boat, which was why it had become so heavy. When he moved his boat, he dragged the other anchor and boat, lock stock and barrel, with him. Obviously he had not realized this and thought he was being pursued by a phantom ship. The event was enthusiastically rehashed and re-enacted at our dinner table and would have remained the topic for the rest of the evening if we hadn't been interrupted by yet another incident.

Our charter guests were still in the dining salon, doing re-runs of what they called the rescue from the phantom ship, when Jules and I had retired to the aft deck. We were both enjoying the quietness of the starlit anchorage when Jules broke the silence and said, "Did you hear that?"

"That tingling sound, you mean?"

"Yes, listen, there it is again!."

"Peculiar sound," I said, "Must be something in the galley."

A few minutes went by and then, "There it is again," Jules said, "it doesn't come from the galley, it sounds as though it comes from somewhere up in the rigging."

I looked up, straining my left ear towards the direction of the sound, which was just then repeated again. "You're right," I agreed, while getting up and moving in the direction from where the sound had come.

We both moved forward looking upwards into the rigging of the main mast. When we came closer we could see a shape, a silhouette of a mast and spreaders, not ours! The spreaders touched our shrouds ever so slightly. Every once in a while, a slight movement caused the metal to rub together, making a tingling sound.

"There's a boat along side," exclaimed Jules. "It's that bareboat again, I thought you had moved it."

"I have," I replied, "we moved it well away from here. It couldn't have drifted back here. It's securely anchored and couldn't possibly drag against the prevailing wind and current."

Our commotion had alerted the charter guests who had now left the saloon and stood on deck watching the apparition. The boat was along side but was not tied. What kept it in its place was her rigging which was caught in ours. I went on board the boat to investigate. It was identical to the other two we had encountered earlier that evening. A rope hung down from her bow. The anchor was not on deck. Our guests hung over *Ring's* railing, curiously looking down at me, moving around on the foredeck of the smaller yacht.

"Have we caught another one?" one of them asked.

"This is better than fishing," someone else said.

"Better call the crew," I urged Jules. "This is a different boat. I guess we'd better move it and anchor it with the other one."

In short order, the crew had moved the shore boat in position and we towed yet another boat to anchor in the vicinity of the first catch.

"Soon we'll have a whole fleet!" remarked Jules laughingly when we came back on board.

"The entertainment is yet to begin," I said, joining our guests who were gathered on the aft deck.

"There's more to come? How can you top this?" one of our guests exclaimed, as if I had arranged the whole proceedings for their benefit.

"Well," I replied, "I bet that those people who belong to these boats are having dinner in the restaurant of the resort on shore. Eventually they'll be going back to their boats, but since they are no longer in the place where they think they should be—" There was no need to finish my suggestive notion. Speculation ran amok.

"But it'll be too dark for us to see anything," one remarked.

"That makes it even more intriguing," another offered. "They'll be using flashlights, and we should be able to hear the outboard motors of their dinghies when they search the anchorage."

That's exactly how it happened. The first dinghy appeared about an hour after we, full of anticipation and armed with after dinner drinks, coffee and deserts, had congregated on deck. Bets were taken on how long it would take each searching party to find their respective boats. The dinghy could be heard as its motor purred, slowly pushing its occupants through the anchorage. Several flashlights directed from the small boat scanned the various yachts lying at anchor. Stops were made here and there when the identity of a look alike craft was investigated. Conversations with other persons on boats followed. Then off to the next one. We were anchored some thousand feet from the resort. We could see the dinghy come closer and closer as the anchorage was methodically searched. With sounds carrying long distances over the water, we could hear the agitated conversations that went on amongst the dinghy's passengers.

"I'm sure we anchored more over in that direction."

"No, no, it's further over there."

"I thought we were anchored closer to the resort," a third voice added.

They were now within a hundred feet of *Ring*.

"I don't remember being anchored this close to that big yacht," another voice commented.

"You know what I think?" a female voice interrupted. "Our boat's been stolen!"

Just at that time, Jules announced that another dinghy, moving in erratic fashion, had left the shore. "That must be party number two," she conveyed to us onlookers. Sure enough, in the distance another dinghy started to follow a similar pattern to the one which was now within hailing distance.

"You have to do something about this," Jules said to me. "You can't leave those poor people wander about the anchorage all night long."

"No, you're right," I agreed, "This has gone on long enough. I'll take care of this first lot. By the time we've got them straightened out, the second dinghy should be close enough to get them organized.

I climbed into the shore boat, started the motor and putt-putted over to the nearby group of lost sailors.

"Hi," I said, "let me take you to your boat."

"You know where our boat is?"

"Yes, it's one of two which were adrift. Just follow me."

I explained to them what had happened and guided them to where the beginning of our fleet was anchored. With great relief they climbed on board. "No, I do not want to come aboard for a drink. Thanks just the same. Have to tend to the other one. Bye! Enjoy your vacation."

Just before I turned in for the night, I heard the singing again. It came from the boat which had been chased by the phantom bareboat. They were still at it. Boy, those drinks Jules served must have been a mighty powerful rum punch!

The Pock

Most people are so involved in their daily routine of work related affairs that it usually takes them a bit of time to unwind when starting their holidays. As a rule, once the sails go up and the boat settles on its course for the new destination, the guests relax and leave their sorrows behind. The movement of a yacht or ship, combined with the disappearance of the shore line, physically and symbolically detaches oneself from the daily routines associated with life on land. This is probably why cruise ships are chosen by many as a favoured holiday. Because of its more intimate atmosphere, this magical moment of almost instant relaxation upon departure, is even more prevalent on a private yacht. The odd time, however, we have encountered the odd soul who had trouble leaving his corporate affairs behind, no matter what!

The Pock, or Pock, as we nicknamed him, was such an individual. His charter group came on board when David Collyer was still on *Ring* and before there were any female members amongst our crew.

The Pock, whose passport stated him to be Peter Pocklington from Edmonton, Alberta,

Canada, was the owner of a car dealership in Edmonton. He possessed several other financial interests and was a self-made man who had done very well for himself. Some years later, Peter became well known in Canada when he ran as a contender for the office of Prime Minister. To sport fans he is known as the owner of the Edmonton Oilers, Edmonton's hockey team, which produced the hockey star Wayne Gretzky.

Peter was welcomed on board with three male friends and their wives and a dark haired, awesomely attractive, knock out of a girl, by the name of Kate. Kate was Peter's girlfriend. One would have thought that, with this beauty at his side, Peter would have forgotten about his financial empire. Alas, that was not the case. Peter's life revolved about units. Apartment blocks or property owned, were units. Automobiles on the car lot, ordered or sold, were units. Kate was a unit, although in her case, most definitely unit numero uno, with a capital U for unit.

As soon as Peter's party came on board, Peter asked me what sort of communication devices we had on board that would allow him to remain in regular contact with his office. When I showed him our radio equipment which was located in the chart room, he was satisfied and asked me to put a call through to his office. When contact was made, he asked his manager how many units had been sold during his absence and left instructions with his office how to contact him in case of emergency. I thought that once we were underway, Peter's interest in the unit figures would wane, but I was proved wrong because the calls were placed on a regular basis during all hours of the day and often late at night. The results of the day's sales became a regular topic of conversation during the trip. Often, at days end, I would jokingly ask Peter how his day at the office had been. Depending on the amount of units sold, Peter would either be cheerful or shake his head with a frowned face. No matter what we tried, none of us could shake Peter loose from his business enterprise. Peter was a fun guy to have onboard, but his inability to untie the mooring lines from his business started to bother me. Besides the nuisance of repeatedly having to spend much time trying to establish radio contact with the Miami telephone operator, which is a very busy circuit, I felt that the charter trip could not be fully enjoyed unless Peter could let go and give way to a truly relaxed vacation.

During this charter there was some international tension due to some unsettling events taking place in Cuba. This, besides the units, was very much the main topic of conversation amongst my guests. Every evening, just before dinner time, I would put on the head phones and tune in to the news on our short wave radio transceiver. I would then report the results to the charter group. This evening ritual gave me the opportunity to shake the very foundations of Peter's contact with his Canadian based operation.

The dinner table was set. The candles were lit and the charter party was seated. The entrée had not yet been served. The dinner party was chatting, making idle conversation. I was in the chart room listening to the news. When the announcer had finished, I turned the radio off and put the head phones down. I walked to the dinner table to take my seat. Expectantly, the guests looked at me, waiting to hear an update of the news. Instead, I asked Aubrey, our steward, to start serving dinner. Conversation, somewhat haltingly, re-started. Except for the occasional dinner-related small talk such as, "pass me the salt please," I remained fairly subdued and quiet. After a few minutes had gone by, Ian, one of the guests, looked at me and asked, "You seem depressed, is there a problem?"

Not too convincingly, I answered, "No, everything is fine."

The manner in which I had answered was noted by everyone seated at the table. I noticed the exchange of a few glances and a shrug. A few more minutes went by, when again Ian said, "Come on, Jan, what's the matter, why are you so quiet?"

"It's—eh—it's nothing, I'll tell you after dinner."

This really started the ball rolling. Now everyone wanted to know what was on my mind. Pressure was being applied by the entire group to spill the beans. David Collyer, who was seated beside me, gave me a look of, "what's he up to now?" I discreetly kicked his leg under the table, signalling him to keep quiet. To the guests, I pretended to give in reluctantly. I scraped my throat and began telling my devious lie.

" I didn't want to spoil your dinner, but if you insist, I'll tell you now. I have just heard the latest news and it's really bad."

Momentarily, I studied the party at the table. Their facial expressions indicating concern, cutlery held motionless in their hands, they gave me their undivided attention.

"The situation in Cuba has not been resolved and the United States and Russia are now at war."

The announcement hit like a bomb. Agitated conversation started around the table. "I knew it," one of them said. "It was to be expected," another one added. I let them speculate on my news item for a few minutes then I said, "There's more!"

The group quieted down.

"All international flights have been stopped. All communications on an international level have been stopped as well."

I looked at Peter who was sitting opposite me at the other end of the table. I saw his chin drop. Dismayed, he gazed at me. I could almost see his brain checking off the units which would leave his showroom without his knowledge, or worse, would not be sold as a result of the uncertain future. I continued my message of doom.

"I have given this situation some thought. Returning to Canada appears to be out of the question. It seems quite obvious that you'll have to remain here for an undetermined amount of time. Here, in the Caribbean, we should be relatively safe. Under the circumstances, it would be best if you remain on board, which you're quite welcome to do, since my next charter groups won't be able to get here anyway."

This remark prompted a lot of agreeable

comments from around the table. I continued, "I assume that supplies will soon be difficult to obtain since most food stuffs are imported from the U.S. and Europe. Therefore, I think it would be best if we set course for the nearest large port to stock up on provisions." Again, this comment was received with agreement. "You are presently charter guests," I resumed. "You have paid for this cruise, and I think it would be fair to continue on that basis until we come to the end of the charter term. After that, you will have to pitch in wherever needed and together we will have to make the best of it."

This started a lively discussion mixed with speculations and opinions of what the future would bring. The various pros and cons were analyzed and deliberated. I began to get the impression that to some the situation became quite acceptable, an adventure, almost. Aubrey was serving desert when I asked for everyone's attention once again. Obediently, the contingent listened.

"This situation gives rise to one other problem."

Questions appeared on the faces of my audience.

"I have an all male crew on this vessel. In fact, including yourselves, the males outnumber the ladies, eleven to three. This could become a difficult situation if we have to remain at sea for a long time."

David choked on a spoonful of desert. I gave him another kick under the table. The expressions on the faces of my guests turned to puzzled concern.

"Under the circumstances, you should expect that as time goes on, it may be necessary to start a rotation system whereby the ladies are shared equally amongst the male complement." Then I quickly added, "And since I am the captain, I will have first pick, so Kate," I pointed at Peter's beautiful companion, "you'll sleep with me tonight!"

For a moment there was dead silence. Then someone started to chuckle until everyone broke out in laughter. Peter had been very quiet, but now fully recovered he exclaimed, "You son of a gun, you really had me going there. You had us believing everything you said. This is one dinner I'll never forget!"

He never did. Nor did he make any further radio calls. I think he realized that his business would survive without him for a while.

Peter returned to *Ring* again for other charters, this time married and accompanied by his charming bride Eva. Later, Eva and Peter travelled the Virgin Islands with us in the company of their children and my daughters, Michele and Karen, who had flown down with the Pocklington family from Edmonton. Whenever I see Peter and Eva, the subject of the war is bound to come up sometime during the conversation. As he said, he never forgot.

Next time I see him, I must ask what happened to Kate. I'll never forget her!

One of The Big Ones

The sport of fishing has never held much attraction for me. While it may be exciting to watch the rod jerk when a fish grabs the hook and while it may get the adrenalin flowing when the wretched creature is pulled from its element, I can't help but feel sorry for its desperate antics of struggle for freedom. When underway with *Ring*, it was usually the crew who would rig up the fishing gear and set a line or two to be towed behind the stern. Often, a fish was caught, usually a bonito or barracuda. The bonito we would keep, clean and eat. The barracuda would be eaten too if it was caught in the right area. For some reason, barracuda caught in the vicinity of Antigua can be poisonous. Experts attribute this to copper deposits in the bottom of the sea in that area.

The odd time we would catch a dorado which is locally called a dolphin, not to be confused with the porpoise. The dolphin, known in Hawaii as a mahi mahi, is a flat nosed fish with beautiful colouring. As the fish dies, it loses its brilliant colours. It reminds me of the sun disappearing beyond the horizon after having given a magnificent display of final salute to the expiring day.

Catching a dolphin, or mahi mahi, bothers

me. These fish appear to be travelling in pairs. male and female. A story related to me by Hugh and Suzie of the sailing yacht *Captiva* gives me nightmares whenever I see a one of those creatures laid out on the counter of a local fish stand.

Hugh and Suzie were crossing the Indian ocean and had set out a line to catch a fish. The fish they caught was a dolphin. It was caught shortly before dusk. Happy with the catch, they brought the fish on board. When Hugh clobbered the fish over the head to relieve it from its misery, Suzie caught sight of the creature's mate near the water's surface at the stern of the yacht. It appeared to be looking for its friend, husband, wife, or whatever. It gave Suzie a bit of a chill but soon she lost sight of the fish when darkness set in.

That evening they dined on a portion of the fruits the sea had delivered. The rest was put into the refrigerator for consumption the next day. The next morning, after daylight had returned, Suzie noticed to her horror that the other dolphin was still following. The fish swung back and forth in the wake of the boat. Suzie felt certain that its eyes were trained on the stern of their vessel. The fish followed them for eight days, after which they reached Durban which was the yacht's destination. Neither Suzie nor Hugh had been able to make themselves eat the remaining portion of the fish which had been set aside in the fridge.

Ever since Hugh and Suzie related this story to us, I have kept an apprehensive watch on the type of fish caught on our boat. When at one time, to my displeasure, the crew triumphantly reeled in a dolphin, I immediately cast an anxious eye upon the waters behind our stern and sure enough, there was the other one following! With alarm, I told the crew to release the fish which was dangling from the line as it came on board. The crew did as I wished, but must have been convinced that their skipper had gone bonkers.

As a rule, our guests paid attention to our fishing line only when a fish was caught. Everyone would gather around to come and see the fish as it lay wriggling on the decks. The odd time, their interest would be aroused to the point that they might even take the rod from its mount and hold it for a while. Usually, after some fifteen minutes, they would put it back and pay no further attention, except that time when we had one really eager beaver amongst the party. He stood there with the rod, staring at some distant point behind the ship, waiting for action for hours on end. The fishing was not very good at that time; perhaps the fish were too smart or did not like the fellow.

It so happened that this same group kept playing practical jokes on each other. A rubber chicken which they had brought with them played a big part in their entertainment. The stupid looking thing kept showing up in bunks, p.j's, house coats, purses, and even at one time on the dinner table concealed in a vegetable dish. Eventually, the chicken had played all the tricks it could and ended up in our generator room, abandoned. Thinking of my fisherman guest, who had been standing on the aft deck for several hours with fishing rod in hand, I figured it was time to revive the rubber chicken, which by this time had been completely forgotten. I waited until my guest passed the rod on to one of his friends to make a visit to the bathroom. I grasped the opportunity to thread the chicken onto the hook and reset the line. Just before the guest made his reappearance, one of his friends slightly released the tension on the line, to which the reel responded with a sound readily recognized by fishermen throughout the universe. Zzzt, Zzzt, our victim heard the noise while climbing the stairs leading up to deck level. He ran towards the stern and grabbed the rod from his friend. He started to reel in the catch with great difficulty. The thing was heavy. "It's a big one!" he yelled excitedly. "I don't think I can reel him in right away. I'll have to play him a bit until he tires out!" He started playing his prey while at the same time offering a running commentary. "Mustn't reel it in too fast. Must keep tension on the line, otherwise he'll take off and break the line." He reeled in some more. Suddenly, the thing hit the surface of the water and skipped on the waves, then went under again. This happened a good distance away from the boat. "Did you see that!" he yelled, still not recognizing the object. "Boy that's a big one!" The rod bent as the chicken disappeared below the surface, increasing the tension on the line. We had seen it, and were in agony, trying not to burst out in laughter. Fortunately, he had no time to pay attention to the group which had assembled behind him.

Finally, after a good twenty minutes of intense labour, the victim was hauled on board.

It was not recognized for what it was until it broke the water for the last time, close under *Ring's* stern.

Fishermen reputedly talk about the big one which got away. The biggest fish I have ever seen was caught and did not get away.

We dropped the anchor in Saline Bay, a pleasant anchorage off the shores of the island of Mayero. To enter the bay, one has to be careful to not hit the reef which extends for about a hundred feet or so from the northern point of the bay. A British Naval vessel struck this reef during the first world war and its remains, still resting on the reef, are a favourite attraction for divers. As we entered the bay, I spotted the yacht *Snark* resting at anchor. The *Snark* was a charter yacht operated by Gilbert and his wife, Ramonde. Gilbert had been a musician in France. He and Ramonde had built the boat themselves and were now operating their vessel in the charter business. Gilbert was an avid diver and spear fisherman.

After our anchor was securely set and our shore boats had been launched, I decided to take one of the boats for a spin and say hello to Gilbert and Ramonde. When I came closer to their yacht I became aware of a tremendous amount of activity on *Snark's* decks. Lines were being strung, floats were being attached. Spear fishing equipment and diving gear were being readied. In the midst of all this equipment was Gilbert who was frantically moving about and giving instructions to his charter guests and crew. When I came alongside and asked him what was going on, he made it obvious that he had no time to talk. "Beeg feesh, beeg feesh," he kept saying in his French accent, while rushing about sorting out equipment. "I weel see you later. No time now!"

Wondering what Gilbert was up to, I returned to the *Ring Andersen* and my guests. Once back on board and after being drawn into a conversation with my charter guests, I soon forgot about the activities I had witnessed on *Snark* .

The next morning after breakfast, our guests and Jules embarked for the fabulous beach of Saline Bay. Jules went along to act as guide during a short excursion to the top of an adjacent small mountain, from which a breathtaking view of the Tobago Cays could be enjoyed. Upon their return, we raised the anchor and headed for nearby Union Island. *Snark* had apparently already departed in the wee hours of the morning as the yacht was nowhere to be seen. We caught sight of her when we entered the anchorage of Union Island. *Snark* was tied up at the jetty of the Union Island hotel and restaurant. On the *Snark's* decks, hanging from the main boom, was the largest fish I have ever seen. The fish was a grouper, some eight feet long, weighing well in excess of six hundred pounds. I had no idea they could grow that large. The biggest grouper I had ever seen before this was about two feet in length. Gilbert proudly explained to me that he had discovered the beast in a cave in the reef where it probably had been living for a great number of years. He estimated that the fish might well have been several decades old. To me, it looked like a prehistoric specimen that somehow had survived the ages of time. Regardless of my fondness for

The Beeg Feesh

Gilbert and Ramonde, I felt sad for the senseless end of this magnificent creature's life. What for? What sport? The creature had been lying undefended in the cave, its home. It took a man with a couple of spear guns to shoot it dead as it lay there waiting, innocently. The only challenge was to drag the carcass from the cave and hoist it on board with the aid of block and tackle. Surely, for food it was not needed or wanted, its flesh being tough and inedible.

Regardless of my personal feelings about fishing as a sport, some charter yachts are built and outfitted especially for that purpose. Problems may arise which are special to that type of operation.

As the sport fishing boat *Bahari* sped out of the harbour of St.George's, Grenada, the British Admiral, R.N., retired, sat ponderously in the fighting chair. He was much overweight and suffered from high blood pressure. His remaining strands of hair clung to his sweating forehead. It was hot and he was in a bad mood. With difficulty, he pulled a handkerchief from his pocket. As he wiped his perspiring face, he nodded to a liner riding at anchor in the harbour approach and said, "I say Skipper, what ship is that?"

"That is the *Bremen*, Admiral."

"The *Bremen*?" The Admiral shook his mighty head. Disagreeably he spluttered, "Can't be. I sank her in 1915."

"This is a different ship, Admiral. The one you sank was a battle ship— this is a liner— with passengers."

Agitated, the Admiral dismissed the argument

with a wave of his hand.

Martin, skipper of the sport fishing boat, shrugged his shoulders and proceeded on his way to the flying bridge where he joined the helmsman. He was not happy with his charter. The ancient warrior was obviously not in good health. It looked as though the old codger was ready to expire at any time. Martin really did not want this demise to happen while the man was on his boat. Heaven forbid! He shuddered at the thought of all the rigmarole and formalities one would have to go through when arriving back in port with the remains of a dead Admiral.

Yesterday, the Admiral had arrived on the dock and had stated his desire to hook 'one of the big ones'. He was accompanied by his wife. They were staying in one of the hotels on the island and had arranged for the charter of *Bahari* through a travel agent before their departure from England. One glance at the Admiral and his consort had convinced Martin that the couple would be more at ease in the air conditioned comfort of their hotel, than on the unshaded, pitching deck of his craft. The Admiral stood on the dock, huffing and puffing in the blazing sun, speaking to him with short bursts of breathless speech, while constantly dabbing his balding pate with his hankie. The warrior's wife, who reminded Martin of the battle ship the Admiral had served on, stood firmly planted next to his lordship. She was a large woman. Her hair was straight and cut in a bob, like the head mistress of a girl's boarding school from the 1930s. A purse dangled from the crook of her elbow. She glared at Martin with an authoritative eye, the other one being obscured by the reflection of a lorgnette which she held firmly grasped by its handle.

"Yes," she repeated after the Admiral, "one of the big ones." With her free hand she waved at her surroundings and said, as she wrinkled her nose in disdain, "We have been in this god forsaken Colony long enough."

"This island is no longer a colony, Ma'am," Martin corrected her.

"That, young man, is a matter of opinion." She lifted her lorgnette temporarily, giving the skipper a broad glance. "Nevertheless, let's get this ghastly business over with quickly. You take us to where those creatures live. Henry here will catch one and than we can go back to civilization."

Martin tried everything he could to get the couple to change their mind. He pointed out to them that when his craft slowed down to trolling speed, the big swells of the Caribbean sea would make his boat a very uncomfortable place to be. It would also be hot, very hot, since they would be fishing on the leeward side of the island which is sheltered from the wind but not from the swells. But the admiral remained adamant. He had hunted lions in Africa and tigers in India; now he wanted a marlin and that was that. Her ladyship did not particularly want to shoot, hunt or catch anything. She just wanted to let the old boy have his way so she could get back to her bridge club in jolly old England. Martin reluctantly agreed to have the boat ready for boarding at 1000 hours the next day.

Bahari had reached the area where the marlins run. The engines were throttled down and the boat began to pitch and roll. The diesel and exhaust fumes from the idling engines now lingered in the almost breathless air. Occasionally they descended on the eccentric couple and enveloped them with their nauseating smell. Madam stood behind her husband, her hands squeezed into the back of the fighting chair. Her face was set in a determined expression; her eyes were fixed on some distant point near the horizon. The Admiral was strapped into the chair, the sweat pouring from his face, his shirt sticking to his perspiring body like a wet bathing suit. Every now and then he exhaled with short puffs through his mouth, causing his chubby cheeks to quiver as a duck in a muddy pond.

While the deck boy was busy preparing the fishing gear, Martin hovered within the vicinity, watching the Admiral's antics with alarm. He waited until the fishing rod was handed to his troublesome guest and then reluctantly climbed the ladder to the flying bridge to take his position at the wheel and engine controls. As he was about to sit down in the helmsman's seat, he suddenly noticed the Admiral dropping the rod and collapsing in his chair. With two giant strides Martin descended the stairs and jumped onto the aft deck. He quickly released the webbing which pinned the Admiral in the chair and started rubbing the man's hands vigorously. From the corner of his eye he saw the Admiral's wife calmly inspecting the contents of her purse and having found what she was looking for, she walked with resolute steps towards the cabin door, opened it and disappeared inside. A moment later she reappeared, holding a glass of water in her hand.

For a moment she stood in the doorway, looking pensively at the scene before her. Martin, who was still desperately trying to revive the Admiral, wondered whether the water was intended for the cool customer herself, or for the patient, whose face had turned a bluish colour. Her Ladyship now purposefully stepped forward, pushed Martin aside and, looking down at her husband, exclaimed,

"Bloody hell, Henry, all of your life you have been a belligerent old goat, why can't you even die gracefully?" With this remark she popped a couple of pills into the ailing man's mouth and held the glass to his lips, the contents of which slowly gurgled inside.

"Right," Mrs. Admiral said as she straightened herself and turned to Martin who had been watching the spectacle with amazing wonder.

"Let's get him inside where he can lie down and soon he will be back to his old stubborn self again."

Martin and his helper obediently helped the Admiral, who appeared to be coming back to life, out of the chair and into the cabin, where with effort, they lifted his heavy frame onto the saloon settee. After they ensured that he was safely established and comfortably spread out, they returned to the aft deck. To Martin's amazement the Admiral's wife was seated in the fighting chair and in the process of securing the webbing. She glanced at Martin and said, "Right then, let's get one of the big ones, shall we?"

A Question of Morals

The Tobago Cays is an area situated about half way between Grenada and the island of St. Vincent. By many it is regarded as one of the most beautiful anchorages in the world. Locally called the Cays, the region spans an area of roughly twenty square miles and consists of reefs intermixed with small islets. Navigation here is tricky and should be attempted during broad daylight hours only. The water is so clear that the uninitiated has great difficulty estimating the depth under the keel. In fact, it is probably better not to look down into the water when negotiating the entrance, because one might panic for fear of hitting the bottom when in reality there may be as much as thirty feet of water under the boat.

The reefs are populated by a great variety of marine life, including an abundance of vibrantly coloured tropical fishes. Scuba gear is over-kill in this area. All one has to do is put on a snorkel and mask and float on the warm water, face down, and gaze in awe at the spectacle that unfolds.

The little islets are sandy with some rocky outcrops. They all have beautiful beaches and are endowed with a lush growth of palm trees, sea grapes and other varieties of tropical vegetation. The area is protected from the big Atlantic swells by a horseshoe shaped reef which acts as a break water. Yet, the trade winds blow unhindered, which keeps the bugs away and the temperature pleasant.

The Tobago Cays are under the jurisdiction of St. Vincent. Close to the Cays and to the south, lies the island of Petit Martinique which belongs to the nation of Grenada. The inhabitants of this sparsely wooded island live off the sea. Most are fisherman and boat builders. Many of the Island schooners, who still ply the waters under sail, are built here. These schooners range up to about ninety feet in length and trade along the islands, carrying cargo and frequently also passengers. Another favourite pastime of the Petit Matiniquens is smuggling.

Because of its remote location, the Grenadian government has had difficulty enforcing the law on this barren and steep island. Furthermore, the inhabitants see themselves firstly as Petit Martiniquens and only secondly as Grenadians. They are known to be an independent bunch, paying little heed to whatever happens in Grenada.

Rumour has it that once upon a time, when a new police chief was appointed in Grenada, the new chief decided that the smuggling on Petit Martinique had to come to an end. He embarked on a small vessel and set course for Petit Martinique. When he arrived at the shores of this smugglers' nest, he noticed a funeral in progress on the beach. In respect of the dead, the chief decided to wait until the ceremony was over. Impatiently he waited aboard his craft. The ceremony appeared to be taking a long time and seemed to have come to a stop altogether. The crowd was waiting for something or some-one. Just as the chief was about to go ashore to find out what was holding up the funeral, a fish-erman sailed by in his small dory.

"Hey there," yelled the chief to the fisherman, "whose funeral is that?"

"It be yours, Chief," replied the fisherman, "if you come ashore!"

According to local reports, the Chief headed back to Grenada post haste and was never heard from again. The smuggling continues to this date.

We arrived at the Cays with a charter party of six Americans. They were very pleasant people, but perhaps a little bit conservative, as could be witnessed by the dresses the ladies wore. In other words, buttoned up, all the way up, which is some-what unusual considering the climate we were travelling in. After all, we were on a sailing yacht in the sub-tropics, not in a tour bus in Alaska. On occasion, I had heard some, "tut tuts," and "oh my's," when we passed another boat and caught a glance of bikinis, or even more severe, some topless vacationers.

I dropped the hook close to one of the islets. We were possibly not much more than a hun-dred and fifty feet from the islet's splendid beach on which some boaters were gathering shells. In the process of getting the boat well secured in the anchorage, I had paid little attention to the party on shore. When the anchor was set, I stepped down from the helm station and noticed my guests enveloped in a serious discussion. There appeared to be something amiss. I joined the group and asked if everything was O.K.

"Not really, Captain," one of the men said.

"What's wrong?" I asked.

"Have you seen those people on shore?"

I looked ashore and glanced at the beach combers. "Yes," I replied, "they seem to be looking at shells, why?"

"They are not wearing anything," stammered one of the ladies.

I looked at the shore party again. She was right. Some wore nothing, a few others had towels wrapped around their wastes in which they appeared to be storing the shells. To me this was such a common sight that, at first glance, I had not noticed.

"I guess you are right." I replied, turning to my guests.

"But that is awful. How degrading. Human beings should not lower themselves to that level. It's rude and-and-even animals are covered with fur!" one of the other ladies cut in.

"Not all animals are covered with fur, Ma'am. Snakes, fish, frogs, crocodiles, elephants, to name a few. Think of it this way: clothes were invented to keep us warm in cold climates. Here, in the Caribbean, that seems hardly necessary. Anyhow, I wouldn't worry about it. If it offends you, don't look at them. In any case, it's almost lunch time. I reckon they'll soon go back to their boat." Throwing them a comforting smile, I went forward to see what was being prepared in the galley. When I returned to the aft deck a few moments later, I noticed the men huddled together, exchanging binoculars, which were trained no doubt on the female components of the people on shore. My lady guests were nowhere in sight. I shrugged my shoulders and entered the saloon, where to my amazement I surprised my trio of prissie, female charter guests giggling and peeking through the port holes with binoculars.

I could not stop myself from asking loudly, "Are you counting cockles or shells ladies?"

The binoculars fell crashing to the floor. I quickly descended the stairs and disappeared into my cabin. During the remainder of the voyage, any subject, even remotely connected with clothing or fashion, was tactfully avoided.

The incident made me wonder about the morals and values of our western society. Many years ago, discoverers happened to find a little paradise in the Pacific. This beautiful island, called Tahiti, was populated by a people who had no need for money, they wore virtually no clothing, and traditionally the sharing of love was a token of their hospitality. They shared their food, belongings and loving kindness, and welcomed the brave discoverers with open arms. In return we gave them disease and priests who convinced those happy people that they were immoral and living in sin. As a result, they were made to wear clothes, for which they now had to work in order to earn the money to pay for them. Everything went down hill from there.

Also in the West Indies, it is an accepted fact

that many women have lovers and babies from different fathers. Men will frequently have several girlfriends, yet this does not appear to present a problem. The children are adopted by the entire family, usually presided over by the grandparents. There is no such thing as adultery, nor are those children referred to as bastards. Come to think of it, there are no orphanages either.

The term and concept of adultery, in my opinion, is an invention of the high priests in collaboration with the bureaucrats of the ancient past. It serves the statistics by keeping track of the population. Having them neatly organized into family units with a common last name allows the authorities to put the population into neat little squares which can be subtracted or added onto with greater ease. All this sums up to power and control.

The human species is by nature not monogamous. Only a few other species are, and the human race is certainly not one of them. Swans, for instance, apparently are monogamous. That means that once they team up with a partner, they stay with each other for the rest of their lives. Should either one of the partners meet with an accident or sickness that causes that partner to die, the other one will never join, nor will it ever have the urge to mate with another companion.

In Ganges harbour of Saltspring Island, in British Columbia, there lives a swan whose mate was killed by a local culprit. The remaining swan has been around for years, always alone, although sometimes seen in the company of ducks, but never with another mate. We all know that this display of faithful bondage with a partner is not the case with the human species. Widows and widowers frequently re-marry, even with the blessing of the Christian church.

On TV and in the movies, we and our kids may be watching the hero gun down and slaughter his opponents in the most gory manner. Hockey players, the kid's idols, beat each other to pulp during nationally televised programs. Watch wrestling on TV and you will notice that the commercials are geared towards kids. All this is permitted and endorsed by the upright members of our society. Yet, during a movie, show one nipple or one naked breast, and the show is X rated and declared not suitable for minors.

When one day I discussed this phenomenon with a music teacher who teaches in a large North American city, he mentioned to me that he had been teaching a group of young children. The subject had been the composer, Tchaikovsky. He wanted to impress upon his adolescent pupils the different moods that were reflected in the composer's music. He asked them to show their emotions as the piece was played. When he came upon a section that portrayed anger, the kids started kicking and screaming and making up the motions of mowing each other down with machine guns with great accuracy. He had trouble getting them to stop. When the music played a love scene and he asked them to show love and kindness, the kids did not know how to react.

Several crawled under a table and covered their faces with their hands.

Obviously, somewhere along the line, the locomotive pulling our train went off the track. Unfortunately, it is still charging ahead and taking us in the wrong direction.

From an economic point of view, tourism is good for the little island paradises in our world. In many other respects it probably is a disaster. Sir Mitchell, the Prime Minister of St. Vincent, once wrote an article which appeared in several papers and which was titled, *To hell with paradise.* In the article he questioned the merits of cruise ships visiting his island. He talked about the invasion of large amounts of people for short periods of time which upset the island's way of life. He was concerned with the exposure of his people to the seemingly wealthy tourists who flaunt their money and jewelry and express their pity for the island people who are considered by them to be living in such poverty.

I think Sir Mitchell made a very valid point. Poverty? By whose standards? After all, the only real necessities in life are shelter and food for the stomach and soul. Shelter means a place to keep dry and sheltered from the weather, which is easily accomplished in the warm climate of the islands. A comfortable home is not necessarily a six thousand square foot mansion with a garage for several cars and all the other luxuries which, when it comes right down to it, we can do without.

Food? The volcanic soil of the islands is so fertile that fruit and vegetables can almost be seen to turn from seed into healthy plants before one's very eyes. The islanders certainly do not lack in talent and imagination. The islands boast an abundance of musicians, artists, writers, poets and craftsmen. We once watched a local production of Jesus Christ Superstar on the tiny island of Bequia. The cast, including the orchestra, consisted entirely of local inhabitants. Jules and I, accompanied by our crew and charter guests, watched the performance. The undisputed consensus was that the production had put the Broadway version to shame.

To some it may be hard to believe, but regardless of our cars, big houses and refrigerators, we are really not superior. Many people in some of the so called third world countries pity us, and so they should!

To be continued.........

Watch for the sequel

"Gone to Come Back"

Soon to be published.

About the Author

Jan deGroot received his formal education in Holland. At age 18 he joined the Merchant Marine and roamed the seven seas until immigrating to Canada. After some years in business, drawn back to the sea, he left for the Caribbean and operated his own charter business. He is now a Marine Surveyor. He resides in Grenada and has a home in Canada. He is also the author of *Buying the Right Boat* and *Tips and Tricks for Boaters*, presently being revised for the second printing. His articles and short stories have appeared in many magazines.